In this groundbreaking work, Antje Wiener presents the first systematic account of the roles of practices of contestation in international relations and global governance. She focuses on the fundamental norm-generative power of practices of contestation—the basis of legitimacy—and maps the changes that a wide range of such practices bring about. In so doing she provides a new way of understanding change, as well as normativity, diversity and cosmopolitanism. It is a must read for anyone interested in these central issues of our time.

James Tully
Distinguished Professor of Political Science
University of Victoria

SpringerBriefs in Political Science

For further volumes:
http://www.springer.com/series/8871

Antje Wiener

A Theory of Contestation

 Springer

Antje Wiener
Chair of Political Science especially
  Global Governance
Faculty of Economics and Social Sciences
University of Hamburg
Hamburg
Germany

ISSN 2191-5466   ISSN 2191-5474   (electronic)
ISBN 978-3-642-55234-2   ISBN 978-3-642-55235-9   (eBook)
DOI 10.1007/978-3-642-55235-9
Springer Heidelberg New York Dordrecht London

Library of Congress Control Number: 2014938990

Springer is part of Springer Science+Business Media (www.springer.com)

Preface

Why a Book on Contestation? This book's theory of contestation is motivated by two recent developments in the field of international relations theories. *First*, most constructivist and liberal researchers in the field of international relations are by and large in agreement that the realist view, which considers states as the main explanatory source of war and peace in a context of international (read: interstate) relations that are merely structured by the principle of anarchy is no longer adequate to understand global governance in the 21st century. Instead, constructivists have begun to examine state behaviour as bound by communities with given identities. In these communities, norms as routinized practices have turned into unwritten laws, revealing specific societal patterns that inform behaviour. Subsequently, those in the know obtain guidance. Yet, does replacing the state ontology by a community ontology really help, given that international relations is practice by actors who move across borders in the increasingly open space that is created through globalisation and global governance? Knowing how to behave establishes security based on modes of presentation and forms of communication in global politics, to be sure. Yet, how do these routinized practices and unwritten norms play out once borders are crossed and contestation kicks in?

This book's theory of contestation seeks to answer that question. It argues that while the recent, 'practice' literature in international relations theory generally takes a cosmopolitan perspective rather than applying a communitarian ideal of world political organisation, the pattern of socially organised communities is problematic. For, by replacing the neo/realist assumption of interstate encounters that are diplomatic at best and belligerent at worst, the liberal constructivist reliance on communities of practice has thrown the international baby out with the bathwater. That is, if international relations are defined as relations among actors of different national roots, the community ontology makes the norm-generative practice of international relations (understood as relations among actors of different national roots) almost impossible. This situation is due to the underlying assumption that norm following (i.e. compliance with a norm) depends on the prior existence of a community providing the social environment that generates social recognition and appropriateness. Absent a community, both become impossible to obtain. The assumption that agents need to be operating within communities of practice in order for competent performance to be recognised by others (Adler and Pouliot 2011) raises two questions: First, how do communities of practice emerge, if not through practice? Second, how is the norm-generative capability of practice addressed by the underlying community ontology?

As this book argues, the community ontology relies on a fixed community. It implies that any contestation about the normative structure of meaning-in-use, which guides actors in international relations as they enact that normative meaning, remains bracketed. This bracketing of the norm-generative dimension of practice forfeits the central interactive potential of contestation as a social practice that is not limited to notions of opposition, questioning or protest, but which also represents the basis of legitimate global governance. This matters for all research in international relations, which seeks to understand change—be it through contentious struggle of social movements, moral justifications or through more formalised practices of contestation such as deliberation or arbitration. Notably, according to this concept of community, contestation may confirm the existence of a community, yet by definition it does not have the normative power to change it.

This leads to the *second* motivation for writing a book on contestation. While 'contestation research' has become an accepted term in international relations (Geis et al. 2010), the concept's meaning and analytical potential remain to be addressed beyond using the term in merely descriptive ways. Consider, for example, the suggestion to distinguish "justificatory contestation" from "applicatory contestation" (Deitelhoff and Zimmermann 2013: 7–8), which by and large aptly replaces the earlier Habermas inspired terminology of "arguing and bargaining" (Müller 1994, 2004; Risse 2000; Deitelhoff and Müller 2005) in international relations theories. The distinction between types of contestation will be of central importance for the range of theories on global governance and global constitutionalism, to be sure. And this book therefore addresses them in detail. Yet, it is not obvious how each of these two types of contestation actually differs from their Habermasian predecessors of arguing and bargaining.

Accordingly, a main concern is that the increasingly popular reference to 'contestation' comes at a loss of conceptual precision. The multiple and broad descriptive application of the concept has led to a thinning out of its analytical potential, especially with regard to the normative power of this social activity and its legitimation potential for global governance. By undertaking critical investigations into international relations theories, this book intends to reverse that process. As a social activity with normative power, contestation still remains to be more systematically explored in order to apply the concept for research that examines contested norms and the related normative change. To recover and establish the *normative* power of contestation as a practice that is norm-generative, because it involves re-/enacting the normative structure of meaning-in-use at any time, the book turns to three *thinking tools*. The tools are conceptual stepping-stones, which are developed with reference to social science theories and public philosophy. They include the normativity premise, the diversity premise and the concept of cultural cosmopolitanism. Overall, the book's bifocal approach, which guides this critical investigation into international relations, considers international relations as interactions that mobilise *individual* sociocultural background experience and thereby re-/enact the normative structure of meaning-in-use (Milliken 1999; Wiener 2008).

This individually diverse mobilisation of experience draws on normative roots (Reus-Smit 1997; Bjola and Kornprobst 2011). As such, it's mobilisation towards contestation leads beyond the habitual application of background knowledge that is activated by mere 'competent performance' (Adler and Pouliot 2011). This distinction brings the norm-generative force of intersubjective practice back as a central concept in international relations theories.

This book was inspired by Jim Tully's pioneering work on Public Philosophy, and moved along through ongoing conversations. The first draft of the manuscript was written during a writing retreat under conditions that were, in the best possible sense, conducive towards thinking (compare Hannah Arendt in Margarethe von Trotta's recent portrait, 2013). The *Geltinger Birk,* a secluded nature reserve on the German Baltic coast, facilitated the combination of walking, thinking and writing—and 'thinking through writing' (Sontag 1967)—that made it possible to bring threads together and think through a theory which had been in the making over the past decade. It follows earlier work about 'contested compliance', for example, in the rather hasty process of enlarging the European Union eastwards, where Eastern compliance with long-probed Western norms was expected without facilitating access contestation in order to negotiate normativity prior to accession. Thinking, then, while beating the weather, is among the most favourable of conditions; working from an enclave without the constant demands, offers and temptations of the Internet. All of which allowed for a period of pure thinking, periodically enriched by interaction with nature, the elements or friendly neighbours, including not least the majestic white eagle, Canada geese gathering for their long haul towards other longitudes, and, last not least, the ever friendly black coots in their ongoing struggle for standing space on a rock protruding from the water right in front of the cottage.

The material for this book has been accumulated through many conversations with colleagues and students. And while it is impossible to name them all some special thanks are due. They include the team at the Chair of Political Science especially Global Governance at the University of Hamburg, including Hannes Hansen-Magnusson, Maren Hofius, Sassan Gholiagha, Jan Wilkens, Julia Frohneberg and Philip Liste, as well as the group of doctoral students, with whom the manifold faces and possibilities of contestation have been addressed in many discussions, and who all read and commented on the manuscript. In addition, I thank colleagues with whom a number of research projects have been developed which reflect the interest in 'contestation' in international relations, particularly Karin Fierke, Uwe Puetter, Antje Vetterlein and Markus Kornprobst; as well as the group of colleagues involved in identifying 'contested fundamental norms' with regard to unbound constitutionalism, especially, Christine Landfried, Hauke Brunkhorst, Stefan Oeter, Urs Stäheli, Sven Opitz, Mathias Albert, Andreas von Arnauld, Michael Zürn, Mattias Kumm, Andrea Liese, Nico Krisch and Markus Kotzur. For offering comments after reading the entire book manuscript I thank Kathy Hochstetler, Anna Holzscheiter, Harald Müller, Jim Tully and Lisbeth Zimmermann. Last not least I thank Maren Hoff, Anke Obendiek, Ines Rerbal, Arabella Liehr, Stella Brücker and Johanna Stolze for research assistance, and

Barbara Fess on behalf of Springer Briefs in Political Science for their support. The book was finalised during a Visiting Research Fellowship at the Centre for Global Studies at the University of Victoria, BC, for which I would like to thank especially Oliver Schmidtke, and where I benefited much from the inspiring interdisciplinary academic context. While responsibility for the contents rests exclusively with me, the book would not have been written in this form without Eni Metzger. Thank you Eni!

Victoria, March 2014   Antje Wiener

Contents

Figure

Tables

Chapter 1
Introduction: Contestation as a Norm-Generative Social Practice

Abstract The introductory chapter presents the argument and the organisation of the book. It begins by distinguishing between contestation as a norm-generative social practice, which—pending on the environment-entails four different modes (arbitration, deliberation, contention and justification) on the one hand, and the principle of contestedness as a meta-organising principle of governance in the global realm, on the other. The principle of contestedness reflects the agreement that, in principle, the norms, rules and principles of governance are contested. They therefore require regular contestation in order to work. To that end, it is suggested to establish organising principles (type 2 norms) at an imagined intermediary level of governance. Thus, the legitimacy gap between fundamental norms (type 1) and standardised procedures (type 3 norms) is filled by access to regular contestation (as opposed to ad-hoc contestation) for all involved stakeholders. To develop the theory of contestation, the book undertakes critical investigations into international relations theories based on three thinking tools from public philosophy.

Keywords Contestation · Contestedness · Organising principles · Access · Regular contestation · Stakeholders · Thinking tools

Contestation is a social activity. While mostly expressed through language not all modes of contestation involve discourse *expressis verbis*. Thus, among the distinct modes of contestation, including justification, deliberation, arbitration or contention, especially the latter does not necessarily involve language. However, all modes of contestation exclude violent acts, which play a more central role in acts of dissidence. In turn, as a social practice contestation entails objection to specific issues that matter to people. In international relations contestation by and large involves the range of social practices, which discursively express disapproval of norms. Pending on the type of norm, ranging from fundamental norms to organising principles or standardised procedures, this disapproval is expressed differently, to be sure. The mode of contestation, that is the way contestation is displayed in practice, depends on the respective environment where contestation takes place (i.e. courts, regimes, societal or academic). Several discursive codes matter in this regard (i.e. formal, semi-formal or informal). Accordingly, four

A. Wiener, *A Theory of Contestation*, SpringerBriefs in Political Science,
DOI: 10.1007/978-3-642-55235-9_1, © The Author(s) 2014

modes of contestation can be distinguished with reference to the literatures in law, political science, political theory and political sociology, respectively. They include first, *arbitration* as the legal mode of contestation involves addressing and weighing the pros and cons of court related processes according to formal legal codes; second, *deliberation* as the political mode of contestation involves addressing rules and regulations with regard to transnational regimes according to semi-formal soft institutional codes; third, *justification* as a moral mode of contestation according to moral codes involves questioning principles of justice, and, fourth *contention* as the societal practice of contestation critically questions societal rules, regulations or procedures by engaging multiple codes in non-formal environments.[1]

These different modes of contestation indicate that as an interactive social practice contestation may be performed either explicitly (by contention, objection, questioning or deliberation) or implicitly (through neglect, negation or disregard). As a *social activity* that involves discursive and critical engagement with norms of governance, whether voiced or voiceless, contestation is constitutive for social change, for it always involves a critical redress of the rules of the game (Tully 2002, 2008a, 2008b; Fierke 2010; Owen 2011). As a *normative critique* it involves an interest in either maintaining or changing the status quo whether through civil society actors' claims-making, the rejection of compliance criteria in international negotiations, the refusal to implement norms on the ground, spontaneous contestation or debating alternative interpretations of norms. To understand how contestation works as a practice that critically redresses different types of norms in international relations, this book develops a theory of contestation. To that end, it conducts critical investigations into International Relations theories for purposes of theory building. This endeavour is based on selected 'thinking tools,' which are derived from public philosophy.

This use of these thinking tools follows Anna Leander's suggestion to derive tools from social science theories in order to obtain a theoretical framework that is "useful" for conducting "empirical research" (Leander 2008: 12). By applying this approach the *theory of contestation* brings critical norms research to bear and contributes to international relations theory more generally. With that in mind, the following draws on social theory and public philosophy to provide the theoretical background, from which to carry out critical investigations about the way contestation is used in International Relations theories. More specifically, three thinking tools have been selected on the basis of three research assumptions, respectively. They include first, the assumption that norms research must by definition entail research on the normativity of norms. Accordingly, the

[1] For helpful discussions which led to identify these four modes of contestation I especially thank Markus Kotzur, Stefan Oeter, Peter Niesen, Mathias Albert and Jan Wilkens at the *Centre for Globalisation and Governance*'s Research Area 4 at the University of Hamburg; as well as Christopher Daase, Nicole Deitelhoff, Klaus Schlichte, Thorsten Thiel and Lisbeth Zimmermann at a workshop on 'resistance' at the *Normative Orders* Cluster of Excellence at the University of Frankfurt/Main 2013.

normativity premise is addressed as thinking tool number one in Chap. 2. The second assumption holds that international relations are located within a global context where formal political borders and invisible cultural boundaries do not necessarily overlap. Therefore, inter-national relations need to be also understood as inter-cultural relations. This assumption is discussed by the *diversity premise* as thinking tool number two in Chap. 3. And the third assumption builds on the norm-generative power of contestation. This assumption is developed with reference to the concept of *cultural cosmopolitanism* as thinking tool number three in Chap. 4. Each thinking tool will be introduced and elaborated in detail over the length of the book, so as to provide the conceptual stepping-stones towards the theory of contestation.

1.1 In a Nutshell

The *theory of contestation*[2] proposes to consider the principle of contestedness as a meta-organising principle of governance in the global realm. Organising principles are conceptualised as entailing an agreement to insert a space for consultation at an imagined intermediary level (between fundamental norms, on the one hand, and standardised procedures, on the other). The principle of contestedness reflects the global agreement that, in principle, the norms, rules and principles of governance are contested *and* that they therefore require regular contestation in order to work. For the legitimacy gap between fundamental norms and standardised procedures to be filled, therefore, access to regular contestation (as opposed to ad-hoc contestation) needs to be facilitated, in principle, for all involved stakeholders. The *theory of contestation* elaborates on this thesis over the following six chapters. It centrally focuses on norms as the legitimating elements of global governance. Notably, norms are not prioritised or valued according to their 'legality (Brunnée and Toope 2010a, b) but according to the perception of their 'legitimacy' on part of norm-users (Jenkins 2008). To reflect this conflict between 'legality' and 'legitimacy' of norms (principles, rules and regulations), the theory of contestation refers to a typology of norms that reflects the degree to which norms are perceived as shared or contested, respectively (Wiener 2008 and Table 3.1 in this book). The norm-users are defined by the broader category of 'stakeholders.' In functional deviation of the more common use of the concept in relation with the principle of corporate social responsibility which reflects a participatory and dialogical approach taken by corporations in reflection of new global business ethics (Senge 2013; Engle 2011), the concept is used here to include those who claim a legitimate interest in a policy. The norm-user or the designated norm-follower is thus conceptualised as proactive rather than reactive.

---

[2] Note that italics are used hereafter to indicate reference to the book, whereas use without italics indicates reference to the theory.

The main normative argument holds that as the organic substance of the "normative structure of meaning-in-use" (Milliken 1999: 231; Wiener 2004: 190) of any governance setting, norms represent the legitimating core of global governance. Given that norms entail a dual quality (i.e. they are both structuring and constructed) they must be contestable so as to both indicate potential legitimacy gaps and to overcome them. Whereas legitimacy gaps are indicated by empirical research, they are overcome by applying the principle of contestedness, which underlies the call for equal access to regular contestation for all involved stakeholders. The *theory of contestation* is intended to provide a manual of sorts to facilitate a starting point for more systematic and large-scale research that takes a bifocal—normative and empirical—approach to norms research in international relations. That is, it aims to move beyond empirical observations about how norms work (i.e. how given norms influence behaviour), and thereby address the more substantial normative question about whose norms count (i.e. who has access to contestation).

In this regard the principle of contestedness is introduced as a meta-organising principle of legitimate governance in the global realm. Contestedness thus reflects the central assumption that is common to the range of approaches to democratic constitutionalism, namely, that in principle, the norms, rules and principles of governance ought to be contestable at any time by those governed by them (Dahl 1971: 4; Habermas 1991; Tully 2002: 218; Forst 2007). While democratic constitutionalism has conceptualised the principle of contestedness as the citizens' right to contestation vis-à-vis the state (Pettit 1997: 63), this book shifts the perspective beyond the boundaries of modern states and addresses the implementation of contestedness as a mega-organising principle of governance in the global realm. By conceptualising the social practice of contestation as both indicative and required in order to establish and maintain legitimacy in global governance the *theory of contestation* proposes a novel way of interrelating the *practice* of contestation with the *principle* of contestedness.

A typology of norms in international relations (Wiener 2008: 66) demonstrates how organising principles are 'wedged' in between fundamental norms at the meta-level and standardised procedures at the micro-level. Given their intermediate position, organising principles have been defined as *type 2* norms—with *type 1* and *type 3* norms at the more visible upper and lower levels (Wiener 2008: 66). While the literature often overlooks the importance of organising principles as a potential stabilising force of global governance and instead engages in rather exhaustive discussions of whether they qualify as a legal norm or not (consider, for example, the debate about the responsibility to protect, see for many Brunnée and Toope 2010b), the *theory of contestation* puts them right at the centre of the agenda of norms research. This central position is owed to the observation of a *gap* between generally agreed and well justified norms on the one hand, and relatively specific and often highly disputed rules and regulations, on the other. As Steven Bernstein rightly notes, "one way to think about contestation is 'the gap between general rules and specific situations'" (Bernstein 2013: 138, citing Sandholtz 2008: 121; Hoffmann 2010: 10).

To address that gap and develop a suggestion of how to fill it, I advance a two-tiered argument: First, I develop a pluralist alternative to the community ontology which is shared by liberal approaches to international relations—including the practice turn literature and normative constitutionalists—that in one way or other aspire to mobilise community values to counter the democracy deficit of global governance. And second, I draw on norms research in international relations theories in order to pursue the normative challenge of how to fill the legitimacy gap that has emerged between widely respected fundamental norms, on the one hand, and highly contested standards and regulations, on the other. Following the central insight from public philosophy that contestedness both indicates and generates legitimacy, I argue that the legitimacy gap stands to be filled (rather than bridged or closed) based on the principle of contestedness, which warrants access to regular contestation for all involved stakeholders. Crucially, it follows from the bifocal approach that while contestedness is a normative meta-organising principle; its legitimation depends on how sector-based organising principles (such as, for example, the principle of equity, the principle of common but differentiated responsibility or the responsibility to protect) are derived through contingent circumstances in selected sectors of global governance.

The bifocal approach is necessary because notwithstanding common global governance institutions accompanied by transnational legal regimes (Buchanan and Keohane 2006; Zumbansen 2012), the normative structure of meaning of today's late-modern international society involves persistent regional and cultural diversities (Onuf 1994; Fierke 2005). Therefore, late-modern global governance requires access to contestation to be addressed under conditions of globalisation and inter-nationality. With this in mind, the *theory of contestation* seeks to offer a principled approach to explore ways of warranting equal access to *regular contestation* for a multiplicity of agents. As noted above, this theoretical proposition is developed from the conceptualisation of legitimate governance which has been developed by the democratic constitutionalism literature, on the one hand, as well as empirical accounts of inter-national relations that suggest operating under the structural condition of diversity in the global realm, on the other. It expects 'inter-national' rather than 'transnational' interactions to be the relevant reference in the global realm and argues that the contestation of the norms, rules and principles of governance is the rule rather than the exception in international relations. The ongoing debate about the legality of norms vis-à-vis their legitimacy sustains the persisting challenge of establishing legitimate and just governance in the global realm.[3] Norms research in international relations over the past three decades documents that point well. And, as I contend in this book, it reveals an angle on the legitimacy problem, which has potential for further large-scale research that combines normative and empirical research objectives. Thus, while in the 1980s, regime theories

---

[3] Compare, for many, Bernstein and Pauly (2007), Brunnée and Toope (2010a), Byers (2002), De Búrca and Weiler (2012), De Búrca (2009), Dunoff and Pollack (2013), Forman and Mackie (2013), Forst (2012), Krisch (2012), Sands (2006) as well as Zürn et al. (2012).

have observed the convergence of interests, rules, norms and decisions in specific issue areas (Krasner 1983; Kratochwil and Ruggie 1986; Young 1991; Rittberger and Mayer 1993), and in the 1990s, social constructivists have confirmed the powerful intervening role of 'taken for granted' norms in international relations (Checkel 1998; Risse et al. 1999; Price and Reus-Smit 1998), the following decade has raised questions about the very normativity of these norms, thus raising a question about whether they hold in light of enhanced diversity and subsequently, contestation in the global realm. The book therefore elaborates on the concept of contestation as a political practice that both indicates and generates legitimacy in inter-national relations. Prior to developing the argument in detail, the remainder of this chapter defines the leading concepts including the distinctive use of 'International Relations theories', 'international relations' and 'inter-national relations' on the one hand, and the concept of contestation, on the other; and then presents the leading argument, approach and the organisation of the book.

1.2 Inter-National Relations: Theory, Field of Enquiry and Practice

For conceptual precision and following theoretical triangulation that makes inter-disciplinary research on international relations possible, the following distinctions are applied forth-following and throughout: First, the concept of 'International Relations theories' (habitually abbreviated by the acronym 'IR' in the political science literature) is used exclusively for reference to the academic discipline of International Relations *theories.* That is, the concept is understood to comprise the range of theoretical approaches, which set the context or academic research that addresses international politics, global governance, and world society research.[4] Second, the term 'international relations' is used in order to describe the *field of study,* which is addressed by both International Relations theorists and International Lawyers, respectively. In distinction from the concept of International Relations theories, 'international relations' are understood to comprise the sum of all relations between states or nations, which are located outside domestic contexts. In turn, the third concept of 'inter-national relations' depicts the very *interaction* between agents of different national roots (i.e. including the entire range of agents from individual actors via non-governmental organisations, regimes and international organisations to states). The concept of inter-national relations has been introduced to distinguish the practice (i.e. the actual moment of mutual engagement on the ground) from the academic pursuit of theorising international relations. Notably the concept of inter-national relations as practice is used in the literal and descriptive sense of 'action' (see Wenger 1998; Kratochwil 2007). Considering that the status of

---

[4] For some of the leading textbooks see Brown and Ainley (2005), Burchill et al. (2009), Carlsnaes, Risse and Simmons (2002), Diez et al. (2011), Dunne et al. (2010).

the concept of 'practice' is both central to the theory of contestation advanced by this book, and highly contested among international relations theorists, the following chapters will dedicate some attention to the concept.[5] Despite enhanced globalisation, inter-national relations are on the rise rather than on the decline in 21st century global politics. Therefore, the inter-nationality condition as a constraint for legitimate global governance prevails. This matters especially for the theory of contestation and the relevant modes of contestation.

1.3   Contestation

The *theory of contestation* comprises four main features: First, it includes three types of norms (i.e. fundamental norms, organising principles and standardised procedures); second, four modes of contestation (i.e. arbitration, deliberation, contention and justification); third, three stages of norm implementation (i.e. constituting, referring, implementing); and fourth, three segments on the cycle of norm validation (i.e. formal validation, social recognition, cultural validation). It is suggested that based on these four features empirical research is equipped to identify legitimacy gaps in any selected policy sector of global governance. Each of the features will be developed in detail in the following chapters. The theory of contestation is developed with a focus on global governance as the widest realm of a plurality of normative orders, and with the goal to apply the theory to selected sectors of governance more specifically. To illustrate its application the book explores three such sectors (i.e. security governance, climate governance and fisheries governance).

Probably the most common perception of contestation, albeit not the most cited one, was introduced by Walter Bryce Gallie in his seminal article on "essentially contested concepts", which argued that the meaning of concepts differs according to what a concept does on the user's "behalf" and according to a user's "interpretation" (Gallie 1956: 168). Without going into much more detail about Gallie's notion of 'contested concepts' and its perception across the social sciences, two insights stand out for the theory of contestation as a framework for research on governance in the global realm: First, principles are as powerful as perceived by their addressees (as with the example of Gallie's contested concepts); second, perception maintains or changes the meaning of fundamental principles pending on context. It follows that routinized meanings-in-use of universal concepts need to be taken into account, when assessing the role and impact of universal principles.

---

[5] Compare, for example, the contributions to Adler and Pouliot (2011) who focus and elaborate the "practice turn" in International Relations theories. While Adler and Pouliot as well as Sending work with the "ontology of practice" understood as "competent performance", other contributors warn against this conceptualisation as over-simplifying and cutting out analytical complexity (compare Adler and Pouliot (2011), Bially Mattern (2011), Duvall and Chowdhury (2011), Kratochwil (2012), Sending and Neumann (2011)).

In this critical sense, contestation has generated a range of studies that either began with the observation of a specific contested concept or with the notion of critical practices (see for many Tamanaha 2004; Loader and Walker 2007). To assess the contingent meaning of the respective concepts this research applied a bifocal approach combining normative and empirical research based on the method of "retrieval" which proceeded by retaining the concept from its contested context and subsequently re-approached the concept's meaning through critical engagement with its "own motivating ideal."[6] The present critical investigation into international relations theories about the concept of contestation applies this method.

As indicated with reference to four modes of contestation above, the concept of contestation has been used across the board of academic disciplines. For example lawyers refer to contestation to depict the practice of weighing arguments in the process of jurisprudence (Lessig 1996 and critically Brunnée and Toope 2010a). In turn, social scientists refer to contestation to indicate the struggle of social forces over power in the 19th and 20th centuries (Hanagan 1999; Imig and Tarrow 2001; Tarrow et al. 2001). And critical theorists' contestation involves active engagement with public debate about philosophical assumptions (Benhabib et al. 1995; Sen 2009). The decision to draw on Tully's critical concept of contestation rather than, for example, on Pettit's republican concept of contestability (Pettit 1997) has been made precisely because of Tully's practice-based approach. That is, Tully is interested in the freedom to participate and engage with norms, defining contestation as a critical practice with the purpose of participating in the very process of negotiating normativity. By contrast, Pettit is motivated by the objective of establishing freedom from the institutions of the state and government. Tully's take on contestation is particularly crucial for the purpose of advancing critical constructivist research on norms, for his critical reception of the Kantian regulative ideal juxtaposes the latter with a critical ideal derived from contemporary multicultural challenges of democratic governance. Thus, while also advancing a cosmopolitan approach, Tully's philosophical contestation insists on firmly bringing cultural practice back in order to democratise contemporary governance.[7] And, crucially, according to this approach cultural experience, and the multiple identities generated thereby, are considered as equally foundational for generating substantial normative values and principles of governance as Kantian political practice. As Tully notes, since "citizens themselves are required to accord the appropriate mutual respect for each other's respect worthy cultural differences [...], it follows that citizens must engage in this kind of intercultural and agonistic dialogue. Given the need to test the second assumption of cultural diversity in the

---

[6] For this method see Loader and Walker (2007: 17, citing Taylor 1991: 72).

[7] For the realisation of this claim, see also the project DEMCON: Consortium on Democratic Constitutionalism, directed by Jeremy Webber, at the University of Victoria's departments of Law and Philosophy, Canada, founded in 2004, sponsored by Canada Research Chair in Law and Society and University of Victoria, details at: http://www.law.uvic.ca/demcon/index.htm (accessed 14 March 2014).

course of the dialogue, the dialogue is properly called a '*multilogue*'. Such a public multilogue can be thought of as a reformulation of Kant's ideal of 'public enlightenment' in the face of *cultural diversity*." (Tully 2008b: 39, emphasis added AW).

1.4 Argument and Approach

During the past decade the concept of contestation was used by international lawyers and political scientists alike, who called for more critical research on 'compliance' with global norms.[8] For now, the use of the concept in International Relations theories as well as in International Law (compare especially Brunnée and Toope 2010a, but also Byers 2000) is recalled as the background to which this book's critical investigations will speak. The concept's application with regard to studies of international relations gained momentum when compliance with global norms was observed by lawyers and political scientists who noted "contested compliance" (Wiener 2004; Howse and Teitel 2010; Brosig 2012) on behalf of actors who were expected to comply with fundamental norms of international legal regimes, taken-for-granted norms in international relations and/or with norms or regulations of international organisations. Almost a decade later, the concept of contestation has become quite popular.[9] And, its current remit and scope lead beyond the refusal to comply. While its function has mostly borne more contentious intent than the various deliberative practices drawn from Habermasian discourse theory (Müller 2004; Risse and Kleine 2010; Diez and Steans 2005), the increasing use of the concept in situations where anything from friendly deliberation to strategic contention may be implied, runs the risk of undermining its conceptual depth and, as it were, its analytical teeth. To counter the risk for the concept to loose analytical clarity due to unspecified use, this book undertakes a critical review of the concept regarding its use in International Relations theories. By doing so, it assesses the role and resonance of contestation as a concept rooted in public philosophy and brought into international relations theories. The book therefore draws on public philosophy in order to perform critical investigations into International Relations theories (Brown 1992). The decision to focus on the concept in a book-length treatise has been motivated by a concern about "speculative" theories (Brown 1992) that are often compiled in a magpie fashion, i.e. picking attractive bits from other theories and importing them into International Relations theories. This observation stems from the common practice of

---

[8] Compare especially Deitelhoff and Zimmermann (2013), Howse and Teitel (2013), Howse (2012), Teitel (2013), Wiener and Schwellnus (2004), Wiener (2008, 2004); Zimmermann et al. (2013).

[9] This popularity has come to the fore most notably when German political scientists began to adapt the English term 'contestation' into the German language, using "*Kontestation*" rather than the proper translations of "*Umstrittenheit*" or "*Hinterfragung*".

incorporating social science theories into their field, thereby often de-coupling concepts from controversial debates within their root disciplines of political theory, philosophy or social science and putting them to use elsewhere.[10]

Taking into account the two respective theoretical and empirical pillars, it is proposed to work with a bifocal approach that conceptualises normativity and cultural diversity as linked through the very practice of inter-national relations. Accordingly it is argued that the *legitimacy gap* between generally accepted meta-norms on the one hand, and highly contested regulations at the micro-level, be filled by establishing access to regular contestation for involved stakeholders in specific sectors of global governance as an institutionalised routine to counter the potential conflict. This argument rests on the assumption that the legitimacy gap persists *despite* the mushrooming of global governance institutions, transnational legal regimes and global constitutionalisation, and that it is constituted through ongoing inter-national relations when nationally distinct cultural validations come into play. Achieving legitimate and just governance in international relations therefore depends on how the condition of inter-nationality can be addressed in the global realm. The key proposition of the theory of contestation consists in maintaining contestation and thereby bringing the legitimating force of this practice to bear. In addition to providing institutionally warranted access to regular contestation based on the principle of contestedness this proposition rests on the perception of contestation as a practice that is language-based and therefore constitutive for normativity. The argument is developed in more detail over the length of the book.

According to meta-theoretical frames as opposed to eclectic theorising, this book understands International Relations theories to be developing from as well as rooted in social science theories and public philosophy proper (as opposed to incorporating bits and pieces of social science theories into International Relations theories for specific purposes). Accordingly, it recalls the relevant theories and extends them for use in International Relations theories (compare Brown 1992; Albert 2003). The goal is to present and further theorise the concept of 'contestation' beyond the mere denotation of a social practice, in order to maintain and elaborate the concept's immanent impact on social change. For as a political practice, contestation includes the power of defining the meaning-in-use of the norms that govern a political community. Access to contestation is therefore crucial for just and legitimate political order—whether within the constitutional boundaries of nation-states, or beyond. To make contestation viable for the latter, the leading argument consists in reclaiming the conceptual link between contestation and contestedness, which is set by democratic theory (Tully 2000) for international relations theories.

---

[10] While this rather often reflects an implicit if strategic reference to 'imported' principles, a new debate about eclecticism versus meta-theories offers an important critical perspective on this practice (compare pro eclecticism Katzenstein and Sil (2011); for the argument against eclecticism which would support careful reference to conceptual debates in the root context, see Reus-Smit (2013)).

The investigations begin with a twofold query: First, *what is normative about norms*? This question has remained an open query following two decades of constructivist norms research in international relations. And second, it is asked *how to deal with diversity*? This is arguably the most challenging issue for theories of democracy and justice under the condition of inter-nationality. In essence these two questions signify the debate about which role dialogue ought to play in establishing and maintaining just and legitimate political order. 'Dialogue' expressed through any type of peaceful interaction has a central role in political theories of democracy, peace and justice including Kant, Habermas, Forst and Tully among many others. Following the so-called fourth debate among "rationalists and reflectivists" (Keohane 1988; Waever 1996; Christiansen et al. 1999; Fierke and Jørgensen 2001) that shifted towards the constitutive impact of social ontologies, the impact of 'dialogue' has become widely discussed and methodologically refined in International Relations theories (see in particular Fierke 1998, 2010; Wendt 1999; Bjola and Kornprobst 2011). However, the impact of dialogue reaches beyond the consistent constructivist's focus on "rule" change (Fierke 2010: 187). As Tully and others have convincingly argued, dialogue and more importantly still with reference to cultural diversity, "multilogue", transport cultural experience (Owen 2007; Tully 2008a). It is therefore an important indicator for research that seeks to capture and shape normative change. To address this wider constitutive impact of language beyond rule change, then, dialogue remains to be more systematically assessed. To that end, the following chapters focus on contestation as a discursive form of social practice in International Relations theories. The book elaborates on the argument that diversity is here to stay, given that despite ongoing processes of globalisation and regional integration, cultural harmonisation in transnational arenas is likely to remain a rare occurrence. Therefore a more concise understanding of contestation as a way to voice difference of experience, expectation and opinion is crucial. Any work targeting the establishment of just and legitimate institutional and constitutional settings in the global realm therefore needs to understand how contestation works in practice and in theory. With this in mind, the following chapters first address the concept of contestation with regard to the two leading questions about normativity and then turn to elaborate on the application of these normative conditions by empirical research.

1.5 Organisation of the Book

The book's critical investigation into international relations about the role and resonance of the concept of contestation seeks to achieve two objectives. First, it seeks to recapture the critical dimension of the concept of contestation as a dialogical practice that is constitutive for social change. To that end it develops an argument that calls for establishing access to regular contestation in international relations based on contestedness as an organising principle. Secondly, it aims to set the grounds for an interdisciplinary research programme on just and legitimate global governance under conditions of diversity. The programme is based on the leading argument of the *theory of contestation*, which holds that contestation is both *indicative* for sector specific organising principles as norms at the intermediary level, and *required* to establish regular contestation at the referring stage in reflection of the meta-organising principle of contestedness in global governance, more generally. While the two functions will be detailed with reference to the four features of contestation over the length of the book, for now, it is helpful to keep in mind for research international relations, both in law and in political science, that contestation is specified by three conditions: First, given that as a social practice contestation is always carried out in context, it bears contingency with regard to place and time (Tilly 1975; Scott 1988; Jenson 1989). Second, given that as an interactive practice contestation requires at least two participating agents, it bears intersubjectivity (Kratochwil and Ruggie 1986). And third, given that contestation is generally directed towards norms (of whatever type), it is generated in relation with and hence of direct relevance for normative structures of meaning-in-use (Searle 1995: 44; Milliken 1999: 231; Wiener 2004; Bjola and Kornprobst 2011: 11; Giddens 1979). These three conditions of contestation are constitutive for the choice of three thinking tools, which serve as stepping-stones for the following critical investigation into international relations theories: the normativity premise, the diversity premise and cultural cosmopolitanism. The following section briefly introduces each of these thinking tools in turn, thereby indicating their *conceptional* roots in public philosophy.

Following this *first* introductory chapter, Chap. 2 focuses on the normativity premise as the first of three thinking tools. It begins by raising a question about the normative meaning of norms, i.e. what is normative about norms. Drawing on the range of scholarly contributions, especially however not exclusively within the constructivist camp, it notes that while diverse interpretations of norms facilitate a novel and important empirical angle on the role and impact of norms and principles of international relations (Doty 1993; Weldes and Saco 1996; Milliken 1999; Reus-Smit 2001), their impact remains to be explored more systematically with regard to the normative underpinnings of global governance. The chapter then recalls how the concept of contestation in International Relations theory emerged in critical engagement with the compliance literature, especially by norms research that was inspired by the constructivist turn in international relations theories (Howse and Teitel 2010; Teitel 2013; Brosig 2012; Brunnée and Toope 2010a; Wiener 2004, 2008). Its specific use and purpose within the context of International Relations theories, was to facilitate a critical investigation as a scientific practice, which was ultimately spurred by Kratochwil's query of how "norms work" in international relations (Kratochwil 1984). In the process critical norms research scrutinised conventional constructivist approaches that were predominantly interested in the structural impact of norms on state behaviour, and which therefore considered contested compliance as a "lack of fit" that could, in principle, be overcome by using coercion (Börzel and Risse 2000; Schimmelfennig 2000; Checkel 2001). Different from this consequentialist interest in compliance, critical norms research took contestation as an indicator of different background conditions. Rather than focusing on the lack of compliant behaviour with a norm, which was identified by a particular agreement, convention or treaty, this research was interested in diverse experience and expectations as potential causes for different understandings. Accordingly, it took instances of contested compliance as empirical indicators for situations that, if properly analysed, would offer a better understanding of the normative structures of meaning in-use in global governance. As a result, the *theory of contestation* argues, it is now possible to account for diversity in global governance. The argument is developed with reference to the three segments on the cycle of contestation as well as the three stages in the compliance process.

Chapter 3 focuses on the diversity premise as the second thinking tool. It draws on diversity claims following empirical accounts of diversity along the ethno-methodological dimension of indexicality (Garfinkel 1967), on the one hand, and normative arguments about culturally multiverse constitutional contexts (Tully 1995), on the other. This chapter refers to research on governance in the global realm as the terrain where the prospect of establishing and maintaining just and legitimate governance has been considered as the greatest challenge and hence most thoroughly imagined and contested by cosmopolitan philosophers ranging from Immanuel Kant to James Tully. It is argued that Tully's philosophical contestation of Kant's regulative ideal for a political order in Europe on cultural grounds, offers an important angle on the premise of maintaining diversity. The chapter's critical investigation into international relations theories applies the diversity premise to challenge the community ontology. While seldom related explicitly, this ontology is underlying both the 'practice turn' literature (Adler and Pouliot 2011) and normative global constitutionalism (Habermas 2011; Cohen 2012). Its impact comes to the fore as both seek to *overcome* the legitimacy *deficit* of global governance rather than *fill* the legitimacy *gap*. The subsequent claim that contestation is a norm-generative practice is especially innovative for international relations theories because it suggests relating the political contestation of norms back to prior cultural experience. Chapter 3 elaborates on the normative claims of this critique with reference to the features of norm-types and segments on the cycle of norm validation. To that end, it draws both on Kant's regulative ideal and Tully's critical ideal (Tully 2008a, b).

Chapter 4 introduces the concept of cultural cosmopolitanism as the third thinking tool with a view to framing the theory of contestation. This thinking tool is developed with recourse to Tully's "public philosophy in a new key" (Tully 2008a, b). From this background, the application of this thinking tool towards a critical investigation into international relations theories is aimed to identify the interrelation between the practice of contestation and the principle of contestedness. This is done with reference to the feature of three types of norms and their respective degree of contestation (i.e. low, high and regular). Understood as a norm-generative practice contestation is considered as a *sine qua non* for legitimacy in any context of governance, including governance in the global realm. It is argued that to make full use of the concept 'regular' contestation ought to be established as a legitimacy enhancing practice in the global realm. To that end, the *theory of contestation* takes Tully's development of a cultural ideal of democratic governance as the starting point for conducting this critical investigation into the role and resonance of 'contestation' in international relations theories, and thereby propose adapting the practice-based approach to government through civic freedom (Tully 2008a), which has been developed from the perspective of diversity within a national frame for International Relations theories.[11] This method mirrors Jutta Brunnée and Stephen Toope's theoretical move to develop their innovative "practice of legality" approach for "international interactive law" from Lon Fuller's national legal theory about law as reciprocal rather than hierarchical (Brunnée and Toope 2010a: 7, citing Fuller 1969). In sum, Chap. 4 elaborates on the legitimacy gap that emerges between fundamental norms on the macro level and standardised procedures on the micro level. By drawing on Tully's cultural ideal this chapter works with 'cultural cosmopolitanism' as a thinking tool to demonstrate the normative effect of cultural practices in inter-national relations as individual experiences, rather than collective, cultural properties.

Chapter 5 proposes that based on the principle of contestedness (as a meta-organising principle of global governance) access to regular contestation at the referring stage ought to be warranted. This stage is sector-specific and therefore requires empirical research for identification. To exemplify this process based on the three stages of norm implementation, this chapter identifies the referring stage with reference to sector-specific organising principles that are derived from processes of policy-making. This application follows the definition of contestation as both indicative and required for legitimacy. Accordingly, the legitimacy gap that is indicated by enhanced contestation (i.e. when the respective legal and social contexts do not provide for the social recognition which is required in order to accept a norm as appropriate and implement it according to the required regulations) as the 'space' where normative meanings are contested in International Relations theories. By including regular contestation within an institutional (and, pending on the degree of constitutionalisation in a specific context, the constitutional) setting, the potentially conflictive outcome of political contestation when performed either as spontaneous protest, or conducted as strategic intervention, may thus be 'tamed'.[12]

To demonstrate the value-added of this concept, the following Chap. 6 turns to three explorative cases in which the relation between three types of norms is presented through the sector-specific narratives. The cases and the respective selection of norms that play a role at the three stages of norm compliance include security governance (civilian inviolability, responsibility to protect, non-intervention), climate governance (sustainability, common but differentiated responsibility,

---

[11] Note the use of the concept of 'governance' rather than 'global governance' so as to distinguish a pluralist from a modernist approach to governance in the global realm.

[12] For the notion of 'taming' power through institutions compare Peter Katzenstein's work on Germany within the European Union, see Katzenstein (1997).

emissions standards) and fisheries governance (sustainable fisheries, precautionary principle, fishing quotas).

The concluding Chap. 7 summarises the book's objective to develop the theory of contestation by using three thinking tools, and thereby highlighting the inter-relation between contestation (as a norm-generative practice), on the one hand, and contestedness as a meta-organising principle of global governance, on the other. The chapter highlights the central claim of the *theory of contestation*, which holds that by understanding contestation as a critical discursive practice that is consti-tutive for normative change, a constructive contribution is made to the legitimacy 'deficit' debate, insofar, as it facilitates ways to allocate and establish regular contestation in selected sectors of global governance. It shows advances on innovative approach to theorising legitimate and just governance in the global realm under conditions of inter-nationality despite ongoing globalisation.

Chapter 2
The Normativity Premise: The Normative Power of Contestation

Abstract This chapter focuses on the normativity premise as the first of three thinking tools. It begins by raising a question about the normativity of norms. It notes that while diverse interpretations of norms facilitate a novel and important empirical angle on the role of norms in international relations, their impact remains to be explored more systematically with regard to the normative underpinnings of global governance. It then recalls how the concept of contestation in International Relations theories emerged through critical engagement with the compliance literature, especially by research inspired by the constructivist turn in international relations theories. The argument is developed with reference to the three segments on the cycle of contestation as well as the three stages of norm implementation.

Keywords Normativity premise · Norms research · Normativity · Compliance · Governance · Cycle of contestation · Stages of norm implementation

The 'normativity premise' is introduced as the first of three thinking tools, which have been chosen as stepping-stones for the theory of contestation *from* the background of public philosophy *for* the advancement of International Relations theories. The focus on normativity reflects the concern about the risk of 'contestation' to loose theoretical 'teeth' as a concept of norms research as an unintended consequence of its mushrooming application for what turns out to be mainly descriptive purposes. I hold that the more the concept is used to merely describe deliberative engagement that remains normatively non-substantial, the more its analytical relevance is likely to become blurred. To counter this tendency the *theory of contestation* suggests a bifocal approach in proper reflection of the concept's constitutive and normative role. The intention is to re-establish the concept's leading role in the range of approaches under the umbrella of International Relations theories such as, especially global governance theories, global constitutionalism and international law, respectively. Each is briefly summarised in the following.

A. Wiener, *A Theory of Contestation*, SpringerBriefs in Political Science, DOI: 10.1007/978-3-642-55235-9_2, © The Author(s) 2014

Global governance theories emerged in the 1990s and are, in their majority, interested in creating norms with the intention to control the effect of globalised movement of capital, finance and trade through policy mechanisms and international organisations. In turn, global constitutionalism addresses the normative substance and public legitimacy of constitutionalisation beyond the nation state. It has emerged as a new interdisciplinary field in the past decade and is defined as the interdisciplinary theoretical framework to study "unbound constitutionalisation", i.e. processes of constitutionalisation that unfold without being explicitly bound by states (Wiener and Oeter 2011; Wiener et al. 2012). Finally, theories of International Law have demonstrated a concern with the substantive change a norm undergoes over various stages of development from social via emergent legal norms to legal norms (Byers 2000; Toope 2003; Brunnée and Toope 2010a, b and critically; Finnemore 2000). Norms play a central role as constitutive, regulative and evaluative elements for each of these theories. While sociologically speaking they literally express 'normality' or 'taken for grantedness', and are therefore conceptualised as habitual rather than cognitive (Morris 1956; March and Olsen 1989; Price and Reus-Smit 1998), from a legal or philosophical perspective norms carry specific moral weight that establishes their legality through public deliberation (Toope 2003; Brunnée and Toope 2010a; Müller and Wunderlich 2013). And with regard to the constitution of political orders, norms are expected to justify, and therefore, enable public order and authority based on the basic principle of democratic constitutionalism, which holds that governance acquires legitimation through potential critical interventions by those governed by these norms (Pettit 1997; Zürn 2000; Tully 2002; Forst 2007, 2012). While the act of contesting norms within a *societal* context bears the risk of being excluded from the social group that considers these norms as appropriate, for they are 'theirs', contesting norms within a *legal* context e.g. through arbitration or by deliberation about procedural details such as, for example, which norm applies in case of competing legal orders, and how to apply them, or is a routine procedure which is considered as common and therefore appropriate (or 'normal') in jurisprudential procedures (on the rules of 'Treaty Law' compare Chayes and Chayes 1993). In turn, contesting norms within a *political* context involves formalised debating procedures, for example, in parliament or during public electoral debates, as well as public forms of struggle, which are considered appropriate within specific political orders. In all three contexts the 'work' of norms unfolds in appropriate ways, either habitually established or formalised by appropriate procedures.[1] In these contexts and the respective circumstances, the practice of referring to norms bears a degree of 'normality', that is of everyday routine, of which contestation is part. What this chapter seeks to demonstrate, however, is that while contestation may be considered a regular and appropriate practice, the effect of this practice (i.e. the normativity that is generated through it) differs considerably, pending on the respective choice of epistemology and ontology (Kratochwil and Ruggie 1986). The following sections therefore turn

---

[1] For the question of how norms 'work' compare Kratochwil (1982: 686).

to the leading question of what is normative about norms, and explore this question with regard to the literature on norm research in International Relations theories.

2.1   What Is Normative About Norms?

Norms research in International Relations theories distinguishes two substantially distinct positions: For example, an epistemological position that derives norms for a community with a "given" identity (Katzenstein 1996: 5; Adler and Pouliot 2011) will read their meaning off a constitutive script. In turn, an epistemological standpoint that considers norms as intersubjectively constructed, will read the normative meaning off the practice of re/enacting norms (Kratochwil and Ruggie 1986; Wiener 2008, 2009; Wiener and Oeter 2011).[2] The former approach has been summarised as undertaking, perhaps unintentionally, an "ontologisation of norms", which take the substance of norms as given; in turn, the latter approach conceptualises norms as entailing a "dual quality" and, accordingly is interested in both the constructive and the structuring dimension of norms (Wiener 2007: 51; Holzscheiter 2011; Rosert 2012; Deitelhoff and Zimmermann 2013).[3] Importantly, ontological approaches are restricted to the choice of norm while critical approaches address normative meaning. Pending on the respective choice of epistemological position therefore, the practice of norm contestation can have two different effects. On the one hand, contestation may establish which norm is appropriate and how to implement it. On the other hand, contestation is understood as adding to the re-/construction of normative meaning. In the latter case, contestation may either generate changing normativity through critical approval or identify disapproval. All depends on how normative substance is perceived by the respective agents and with regard to each of the three segments that are part of a cycle of potential contestation (compare Table 2.1).

The three stages include, first, constituting norms by establishing formal validity by a political community (international society, community); second, referring to norms as an appropriate indicator of behaviour or a source of social obligation held by a group (regime, organisation or another type of social environment); and, third, implementing norms 'on the ground' (by individual norm-users including policy-makers, public servants, firms, corporations, parties or organisations). The three types of agency are distinguished according to both the segments in the cycle of norm validation and the respective stage of norm implementation (compare Fig. 2.1). The three stages indicate when contestation is possible *in principle*.

---

[2] For epistemological standpoints and their relevance for analytical perspectives that allow for critical investigations into political science and later international relations, compare the feminist literature in the 1980s and 1990s, especially Sandra Harding (1986) as well as Joan Wallach Scott (1988), and for IR, especially Weber (1994), Whitworth (1989) and Zalewski (1996).

[3] This argument draws on Melucci's critical account of the 'ontologisation of social movements' (1988) and on Giddens' concept of 'structuration' (1979).

Table 2.1 Three segments of norms

Segments	Reference	Form
Formal validity	Official document	Law, law-like
Social recognition	Social group	Unwritten, law-like
Cultural validation	Individual experience	Socio-cultural, informal

These three segments are situated on the cycle of norm validation. They indicate the likelihood of contestation as opposed to the fixed combination of agency and segment at a given stage of norm implementation. Notably, at each stage one of three distinct segments of norms is predominantly addressed (i.e. formal validity, social recognition, and cultural validation) (Fig. 2.1).[4]

Each segment on the cycle operates in interaction with the other and with reference to a specific norm. The more an approach is in the position to account for potential contestation, the higher the likelihood to establish legitimate governance. To probe this assumption, the following reviews four major approaches to norms in international relations theories. By distinguishing four rather than two approaches (i.e. conventional vs. critical constructivism), the *theory of contestation* seeks to highlight the crucial importance of analytical standpoints. For example it makes a substantial difference whether norm-generative power is related to the practice of contestation itself (norm-generative power), or whether it is allocated at community level (community ontology). Most recently these standpoints have been advanced by a range of contributions that draw on the philosophy of language and straddle the boundaries of public philosophy, diplomacy and security studies (Fierke 2010; Bjola and Kornprobst 2011). They help clarifying the normativity premise based on their distinctive deontic understanding of practice. To discuss the four approaches with regard to the theory of contestation, each is assessed with regard to the normativity premise (compare Table 2.2). That is, they are compared according to their respective understanding of norms and allocation of normativity.

The distinction on the vertical axis considers the allocation of normativity as rooted either internally (i.e. plural and conceptually contestable) or externally (i.e. universal and normatively given). In turn, the distinction on the horizontal axis notes whether norms are approached from a 'community ontology' or from a 'diversity ontology'. From these cross-references to normativity and ontological preference four central distinctions are notable regarding the functions ascribed to norms: *First*, the conventional constructivist approach in the first quadrant derives the role and recognition of norms from their community environment and the respective normative order that guides that community. Accordingly, norms are

---

[4] I thank Jim Tully for suggesting the cyclic approach to the three dimensions of normative meaning-in-use.

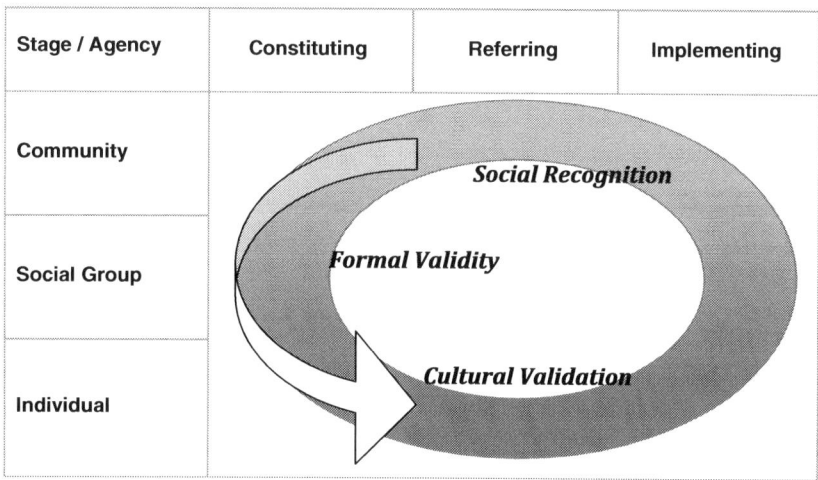

Stage / Agency	Constituting	Referring	Implementing
Community		*Social Recognition*	
Social Group	*Formal Validity*		
Individual		*Cultural Validation*	

Fig. 2.1   The cycle of contestation

Table 2.2   Two ontologies: community versus diversity

Perspective	Community ontology	Diversity ontology
State plus	(1) Conventional constructivist Norms *structure* state behaviour	(3) Regimes Norms *are the glue* of regimes
Global	(2) Global governance Norms *guide and control* multiple actors	(4) Critical/consistent constructivist Norms *form part of* the normative structure of meaning-in-use

considered as standards of behaviour in international relations (Q1). *Second*, the global governance approach in the second quadrant conceptualises norms as principles and rules of a given cosmopolitan order in which their role is to guide, monitor, control or steer governance (Q2). *Third*, regime theories consider norms as the glue of transnational regimes, which develop through interaction in the context of cross-border and transnational institutions and organisations (Q3). *Fourth*, critical and consistent constructivists consider norms as constituted through practice. Norms are understood as carriers of meaning-in-use, which is re-/enacted through social practice. Given that contestation is a discursive practice that critically engages norms, it is the main access point for contestation research (Q4). The distinction of these four approaches has been simplified on purpose so as to shed light on the normative power potentially allocated by each approach with reference to their respective concepts of community or diversity respective. This allocation matters for the normative effect of contestation as a language-based practice that generates change—arguably the most important indicator of the normativity premise. The four distinctions reveal where each approach ultimately allocates normativity with regard to the cycle of norm validation (i.e. which segment matters, which type of actor may intervene and at which stage).

Accordingly the following scale of normativity (based on the insertion of regular contestation) materialises on a range between one (low) and four (highest): Normativity is externally allocated and norms are conceptualised as taken for granted from the standpoint of community ontology (Q1: conventional constructivist); normativity is internally allocated and norms are conceptualised in the same way (Q2: global governance); normativity is externally allocated but norms are understood from the stand-piont of diversity ontology (Q3: regimes); normativity is allocated internally and norms are understood in the same way (Q4: critical constructivist). It follows that approaches, which allocate normativity internally and consider norms as intersubjectively constructed provide the highest potential for contestation. In that case, the decision to establish access to 'regular' contestation with the purpose of establishing or maintaining legitimate and just governance in the global realm would be most plausible. Notably, this discussion of the normative roots of norms is about the larger question of legitimate governance as opposed to the purpose of explaining strategic decisions in the process of governance.[5] As Table 2.2 shows, whether implicitly or explicitly noted, each approach applies specific normative assumptions. The following elaborates on the respective functions attributed to norms. Thus it becomes possible to explore the normative roots of each approach and subsequently establish whether or not the normativity premise is sustained or absent.

(1) Norms as Standards of Behaviour: Conventional Constructivism

Conventional constructivists identified norms as intervening variables in international politics. While allowing for a better understanding of the effect of social group environments and identity on international decision-making this theoretical move has never challenged the role of the state as the most powerful agent in international relations theories (compare for example Wendt 1994, 2003). Accordingly, constructivist overviews have dubbed this approach the "conventional constructivist strand" (Fierke 2010). Based on an interest in explaining state behaviour with reference to regulative and constitutive norms (i.e. taken for grantedness), this research turned towards social indicators to explain commonalities in the behaviour of states (Finnemore 1996; Jepperson et al. 1996). It was first and foremost considered with explaining and/or understanding policy choices (for example about organisational design), political decisions (for example about membership or cooperation) or acknowledging a general acceptance of fundamental principles of international law (such as, for example human rights).

When constructivist empirical research was able to demonstrate that norms have an impact on how states behave in international relations, norms research became a respected trademark approach in International Relations theories. By

---

[5] For these two essentially different takes on academic research compare Cox (1983).

drawing on organisational theory norms were sociologically defined as standards of behaviour (March and Olsen 1989, 1998; Powell and DiMaggio 1991; Finnemore and Sikkink 1998). And Peter Katzenstein and his colleagues convincingly showed that the socio-cultural environment of decision-making in international politics mattered even in the sector of security policy (Katzenstein 1996), thus sustaining the claim that as social facts, norms mattered coequally with material facts (Ruggie 1992), even in areas traditionally considered 'high politics' (Hoffmann 1986). Given this empirically probed impact, these sociological investigations about the impact of social facts in international relations considered norms as having an ontological status. This status entailed a stability assumption, which facilitated a novel perspective of the way norms worked beyond the boundaries of national states, and which mattered in particular for the booming human and fundamental rights literature in the 1990s (see for many Soysal 1994; Keck and Sikkink 1998; Clark et al. 1999; Friedman et al. 2005; Risse et al. 1999). This literature shed light on the effect of norms beyond orders, such as for example David Jacobson's research on "rights across borders" (Jacobson 1996). Given the focus on state behaviour and the ontologisation of norms, the only possible instance of norm contestation stands to occur at the implementation stage (compare Table 2.3). That is, apart from the outright rejection of norms according to the conventional constructivist approach, the intersubjective segment of contestation is not applicable.

This changed with Thomas Risse and others' research on the "power of human rights norms," which explored the way norms worked in both directions, from the outside into domestic polities and vice versa (Risse et al. 1999). By introducing this interrelation between what neo-realists have called "two images" of international relations, i.e. the international and the domestic (Waltz 1979), Risse and his group brought in the critical practice of "arguing" as a normative source of legitimating the politics of the United Nations community (Müller 1994, 2004; Risse 2000). While, in principle, arguing was defined in terms of Habermas's communicative action (i.e. a conversation in which actors engaged in the search of the most persuasive argument and were ready to accept that based on the opponents' shared conviction the better argument should 'win', see Habermas 1988a, b) by including strategic activities of 'blaming and shaming' (Liese 2006; Deitelhoff 2009), the critical dimension of arguing as a intersubjective dialogical practice was undermined. After all, blaming and shaming is conceptualised as a top-down practice, which accepts coercion as a legitimate way to 'convince' unwilling designated norm-followers (Risse et al. 1999). To recover the legitimating normative power of communicative interaction, more and more constructivists took to developing critical norms research more systematically.[6] The *theory of contestation* extends along that latter strand of constructivism.

---

[6] For recent contributions see Deitelhoff and Zimmermann (2013), Müller and Wunderlich (2013); for early critical constructivists see the work of Fritz Kratochwil, Jutta Weldes, Jennifer Milliken, Anna Leander and Chris Reus-Smit.

To summarise, the interest in human rights started two decades of constructivist norms research in international relations theory in the 1980s. According to conventional constructivists the social recognition of norms was conceptualised as habitual rather than cognitive. That is, social recognition demonstrated a sense of appropriateness that was felt and shared based on experience within a social group. Norms thus triggered behaviour that was literally considered as 'normal'. This behaviour hence was distinguished by the "logic of appropriateness" as opposed to the neo-realist "logic of consequentialism" (March and Olsen 1989; Risse 2000). While taking into account transnational social movement organisation and non-state actors' increasingly important part in global conflicts (compare, for instance, Keck and Sikkink 1998; Benford 2011), the "logic of arguing," which introduced the specific emphasis on legitimacy, had little to say on the quality of the norms themselves. Subsequently, the normative aspect of norms remained under-researched, while state behaviour in relation with norms received the main attention from students of international relations. A decade on, the concept of contestation has become popular with international relations theorists including those of Habermasian descent.

(2) Global Governance: Norms as Principles and Rules

The second approach to norms has been developed within the framework of global governance theories that build on the observation of the phenomenon of 'governance without government' as a problem in international politics that stood to be addressed more systematically by international relations theories (Rosenau and Czempiel 1992). Albeit quite diverse, by and large, global governance theories refer to fundamental norms as principles and rules of global (as well as regional) governance, which are purposefully established in order to facilitate the principals' instruments for steering and controlling the agents' policy-making beyond the state.[7] Again, and in line with conventional constructivism (see Q1 in Table 2.2, above), global governance theories do not question the powerful position of states as the principal agents in any substantive—normative—way. While global governance theories include a normative dimension and seek to rescue the power of nation-states under conditions of globalisation and enhanced regime-building given increasingly powerful international organisations, the normative underpinning of the fundamental norms of global governance is not conceived as being subject to contestation but as being universally defined for members of a given community.

That is, normative meaning is not subject to contestation. Norms are ontologically defined as the fundamental principles and rules that enable governments to govern despite the abscncc of 'government' in the global realm. Norms work under the condition of anarchy despite organisational attempts to civilise

---

[7] See for example Hooghe and Marks (1996), Jachtenfuchs (1997), Jachtenfuchs et al. (1996), Jachtenfuchs and Kohler-Koch (1996), Kohler-Koch (1995), Marks et al. (1996), Scharpf (1997), Slaughter (2004) and Zürn (2000).

international relations. The normative roots of global governance norms are therefore external to international relations theories. Normativity is only subject to deliberation among students of global governance in so far as organisational detail and compliance with norms are concerned by international law or politics. It is rooted in and derived from either communitarian or cosmopolitan political theory, respectively. Subsequently, debates among global governance theorists have increasingly become theoretical contestations of positions along "the communitarian/cosmopolitan divide" (Shapcott 2001: 30; Cochran 1999).[8]

(3)   Regime Theories: Constitutive Norms Versus Normative Glue

The observation of states complying with norms, rather than contesting them is among the most common perceptions of how norms work in international relations.[9] Accordingly, the powerful effect of norms in international relations is empirically indicated by observations about state behaviour. This empirical angle on norms reflects an epistemological approach to political science that allocates the motivation for scientific research in puzzles rather than ethics or values (compare King et al. 1994). Accordingly, the question of what motivates states to comply with norms under conditions of anarchy, i.e. in the absence of a government that could enforce compliance based on sanctions, does not come as a surprise. Conventional constructivists explain norm implementation with reference to the 'socialisation', understood as a process that socialises individuals *into* an existing group with a given identity, and assume that therefore social learning in international organisations generates appropriateness (Checkel 2000; Schimmelfennig 2000). If that did not suffice, blaming and shaming were considered the political instruments to enhance compliance through pressure or even coercion applied by advocacy groups (see the previous section). With regard to the potential of contestation as a process that generates and changes normativity, it is important to note that these conventional constructivist approaches work with the assumption that the fundamental norms that are at stake, for example, human rights, democracy and so on, are recognised as just and legitimate, given their status as leading principles in international treaties such as, for example the United Nations Charter. These fundamental norms obtain their legitimation through treaties that are agreed among member states of a given community. Most of them are enforceable through international law or equivalent bodies such as for example the appellate body of the World Trade Organisation.

---

[8] Some theorists without direct links to international relations theories do however seek to bring in contestations about normativity. For example, Seyla Benhabib's "jurisgenerative" approach to cosmopolitan norms of global governance includes "sites of contestation" where citizens interact within a federal context, see Benhabib (2007: 32).

[9] Compare Harald Koh's reference to the observation of an international lawyer, which noted that, "almost all norms are followed by states almost all of the time" (see Henkin 1979: 47, cited by Koh 1997: 2599, and Koh 2006, see also Checkel 1998).

In turn, critical regime theories advanced a more encompassing role of norms 'in context' however. They consider norms as effectively providing a glue of sorts for regimes. As Kratochwil and Ruggie explained, in critical juxtaposition to Krasner's seminal definition of regimes as "implicit or explicit principles, norms, rules and decision-making procedures around which actors' expectations converge in a given area of international relations" (Krasner 1983: 1), this effect stems from the intersubjectivity condition, which assigns a cognitive dimension in addition to the habitual effect to norms (Kratochwil and Ruggie 1986). This crucial insight led critical constructivists to conceptualise the way norms work in regimes as inter-subjective working with the assumption that norm implementation requires interaction among the norm (i.e. as constituted by a treaty or script), the referring agent as well as the implementing agent. In the process normative substance is contested, and as a consequence, norms are likely to be changed (Howse and Teitel 2010). The review of the state of the art on the art of the state conducted by Kratochwil and Ruggie (1986) considers norms and rules as carrying inter-sub-jectively constructed meanings. This normative understanding of norms has been taken up by critical or consistent constructivist research dating back to Kratochwil and Onuf as the two founding fathers of constructivism (Kratochwil 1984, 1989; Onuf 1989). Their work focused on the meaning and making of rules and norms of global order. Subsequently, regimes have also spurred multiple critical investigations questioning the behavioural line of compliance research early on. As Howse and Teitel argue, the technical approach to study compliance mechanisms of transnational legal regimes remained on the level of standardised procedures as opposed to addressing larger normative questions. They find that, "(T)he effects of norms, including legal norms, have an inherent complexity that, as Ruggie explains, defies the positivist aspiration to link norms causally to discrete behavioral acts '(P)recisely, because state behavior within regimes is interpreted by other states, the rationales and justifications for behavior that are proffered, together with pleas for understanding or admissions of guilt, as well as the responsiveness of such reasoning on the part of other states, all are absolutely critical component parts of any explanation involving the efficacy of norms. Indeed, *such communicative dynamics may tell us far more about how robust a regime is than overt behavior alone'*" (Howse and Teitel 2010: 130, citing Ruggie 1998: 97–98; emphasis added AW). To summarise, in addition to the notion of the behavioural effect of norms, critical regime theorists including both international relations theorists and international lawyers have thus emphasised the constructive dynamics that are generated through processes of justification and interpretation of norms and their role under specific circumstances. This constructive and genera-tive understanding of the work of norms adds the constitutive dimension of lan-guage to the mere habitual dimension of conventional constructivist norm research. It follows that for critical regime theorists norms are contestable—in principle—at each of the three stages (compare Table 2.3).

Table 2.3 Where is normativity contestable?

Stage (agency)/ approach	Constituting (constitutive power)	Referring (social group)	Implementing (individual)
Conventional constructivist	No	No	Yes
Global governance	Yes	No	Yes
Regimes	Yes	Yes	Yes
Critical constructivist	Yes	Yes	Yes

(4) *Critical Constructivism: Normative Structure of Meaning-in-Use*

The fourth approach counters "the enduring structuralism of norm research (which, AW) results in a narrow understanding of norms that equates their existence and validity with their uncontestedness" (Deitelhoff and Zimmermann 2013: 4). Instead of taking norm stability as the central analytical strength and working with an ontological concept of norms, this approach conceptualises norms as bearing a "dual quality: that is, they are both structuring and socially constructed through interaction in a context. While stable over particular periods, they always remain flexible by definition" (Wiener 2007: 49). It follows that normative quality is generated through the social practice of re-/enacting structures of normative meaning-in-use (Wiener 2009). In the process, normative meaning is contested based on individually held "background experience" (Hanks 1996: 86; Wenger 1998: 8, 137), which informs a range of distinct cultural validations of normative meaning, pending on the range of socio-cultural contexts that is brought together in a given inter-national interaction. Accordingly contestation is in and by itself a social activity with normative power. This perception of contestation as a norm-generative practice marks a new turn in norms research towards embracing the concept of normativity beyond examining the structuring power of norms vis-à-vis state behaviour and beyond the confines of regimes.[10]

2.2 Where Are Norms Contestable?

The critical (and consistent) constructivist approach works with what is called a 'diversity ontology,' which conceptualises the practice of re/enacting normative meaning as constitutive for normativity. This norm-generative quality prevails, whether the practice takes place within or outside a given community. By contrast, conventional constructivist and global governance approaches work with a community ontology (compare Table 2.2). In the case of conventional constructivism

---

[10] This has been picked up, recently by critical norms research in international relations that note that, "contestation can even generate normative power on its own", see Deitelhoff and Zimmermann (2013: 8).

this perception qualifies practice as 'competent performance' by practitioners as members of a given community of practice who "express and convey univocal meaning for the practitioner and the broader community of practice."[11] In the case of global governance approaches, this leaves norm-generative practice to political interaction, i.e. through norm setting in international organisations and so on. To the former two, practice is constitutive for meaning, to the latter two approaches the practice itself is either meaningful—if it is recognised as competent—or not.[12]

Legal theory and political theory have also noted the crucial impact of such distinct interludes of contestation. For example, Brunnée and Toope have brought to theories international law as "interactive" by detailing stages of public deliberation that contribute to establish the moral substance, and hence the "legality" of norms (Brunnée and Toope 2010a). And, Neil Walker has convincingly demonstrated the increasing need to facilitate "translations" of normative meaning in the context of transnationalisation of international law (Walker 2003). Even though international politics do not necessarily benefit from the distinction of a norm as "legal", given the rising relevance of the legitimacy of norms instead (compare Sands 2006; Howse and Teitel 2010; Kratochwil 2012), the critical contribution offered by the interactive approach to international law is the notion that normativity depends on contingent practices. In turn, Tully has shown in his research on constitution building under conditions of cultural "multiplicity", that if the principle of mutual recognition is accepted as a ground rule for the range of potential political agents, contestation is a necessary condition to warrant democratic legitimacy (Tully 1995, 2000).

An interesting cross cutting theoretical move towards conceptualising argumentative contestation as entailing deontic power has been advanced by the "arguing global governance" approach (Bjola and Kornprobst 2011; as well as Onuf 1989, 2013). While referring to global governance theories, which traditionally work with a community ontology, Kornprobst and Bjola propose taking a 'deontic approach' to recover the legitimating source of contested normativity. Accordingly, they "define *argumentative deontology as a communicative process shaping the status functions and deontic powers that structure how global governance is defined, practiced and reproduced*" (Bjola and Kornprobst 2013: 10; emphasis in original text). With this conceptual move, Bjola and Kornprobst follow Searle rather than Kant and open global governance theories towards a consistent constructivist perspective that focuses on the power of social practice itself. They see two advantages facilitated by this move: First, studying status functions and deontic power positions allows for a better understanding of the way global politics is ordered; and second, "a deontological approach to global governance forcefully brings language and argumentation to the front of the inquiry"

---

[11] Compare Duvall and Chowdhury's critical assessment of that practice concept, Duvall and Chowdhury (2011: 337), see also Bially Mattern (2011: 70–72).

[12] For this ontological understanding of practice as competent performance, see Adler and Pouliot (2011).

(Bjola and Kornprobst 2013: 11). This move along consistent constructivist lines (Onuf 1989, 2013; Fierke 2010) entails a radical innovation for the canon of global governance theories: For it takes a decidedly normative approach of deontological ethical reasoning, which rests the constitution of the normative substance of global governance entirely on language,[13] Agency—understood as deontic power, which follows from assigned status functions—is thus socially constructed. "[D]eontic powers are constitutive of global agency and they prescribe the spectrum of moral responsibilities within which the agent can legitimately function" (Bjola and Kornprobst 2013: 12). By linking the principled debate about the ground rules of global order with consistent constructivist methodology, this approach offers the most concise approach to practice as morally constitutive, so far. While the "arguing global governance" argument approaches contested normativity from global governance theories, two aspects are noteworthy for the argument about contestation as a social practice that is constitutive for normativity, which this book seeks to develop further. First, this approach conceptualises normativity as generated through argumentation, which in turn "provides a fruitful vehicle for understanding moral implications of the deontic powers that come attached to such status functions (as for example, AW) self-authorization, social recognition, political legitimacy, etc." (Bjola and Kornprobst 2013: 12). Second, it focuses on socially constructed meanings that generate understanding for moral responsibilities. The meanings depend, however, on status functions rather than predesigned moral principles or duties. In doing so, it offers an important theoretical bridge towards interactive international law as well as critical norms research.[14] As such, the arguing global governance approach will be recalled in the following Chap. 3 which addresses the political effect of contestation on legitimate and just global governance.

2.3 Contestation as Normative Practice

Building on critical and consistent constructivist approaches the *theory of contestation* distinguishes three stages in the political process where norm contestation becomes possible, albeit for exclusive actorship. Each stage considers a distinct segment on the cycle of norm validation (compare Table 2.3). Thus, the *formal validity* of norm is contestable at the constituting stage (i.e. in the process of drafting of a constitution, a treaty, a convention). At this stage, it is most likely to encounter the deliberation or justification as viable modes of contestation. The *social recognition* of a norm is contestable at the referring stage. It comes to the

---

[13] Compare Erskine's distinction between "consequentialism" and "deontology" as two types of ethical reasoning in normative international relations theory (2013: 44–46).

[14] For the latter, compare Brunnée and Toope (2010a), as well as Deitelhoff and Zimmermann (2013), Kratochwil (1989) and Wiener (2008).

fore most clearly, when different social groups do not agree about which is the appropriate behaviour in a given situation. This is notably the problem spot of the 'spiral model', which struggles to link international push of norms with the absence of domestic pull, resulting in a compliance problem (Hochstetler and Viola 2012, Hochstetler 2012). The *cultural validity* of a norm is contestable at the implementing stage where individuals bring their respective background experience to bear. At this stage it is 'down' to individuals to engage with a norm, for social recognition, which would generate a sense of appropriateness of a norm is not warranted. This type of contestation is most likely in inter-national encounters where unknown agents meet whose respective background experience and normative baggage differ significantly (Table 2.3).

To summarise, given that norms gain 'normality' (defined as recognition or a sense of appropriateness) through reiterated and—notably—interactive use, it follows that the power of norms depends on the degree to which normative meaning overlaps in socio-cultural interfaces (defined as arenas). These interfaces, which I have called "transnational arenas" elsewhere (Wiener 2008) are constructed through practice, and can, therefore be reconstructed with reference to practice by empirical research.[15] That is, they emerge through the enactment of normative structures of meaning-in-use. To indicate where empirical research is likely to identify and verify such interfaces, it is helpful to distinguish three stages in the process of norm implementation and the different types of agency involved. In each of these stages normative meaning is potentially contested. The first stage is identified as the constituting stage of norm generation. At this stage a norm's formal validity is most likely to be contested. The involved actors are most likely to be constitutive powers or their representatives who bestow formal validity to selected norms by signing inter-national treaties. The second stage is identified as the referring stage. At this stage the social recognition of a norm is most likely to be contested. At this stage any type of agent acting in a societally structured context of a community making habitual reference to common socially recognised norms or rules will refer to norms without contestation. In turn, social groups that are not part of the community are expected to contest the norm. And the third stage is defined as the implementing stage. At this stage the cultural validation of normative meaning is most likely to be contested. At this stage individual agents or groups are expected to contest norms, rules and procedures according to their respective individual interests. As Table 2.3 documents, considering the type of agency involved, the four approaches to norms in international relations discussed above, show different allocations of normative contestability. Notably, two approaches provide conceptual leverage to address contested normativity at stage one (i.e. global governance and critical constructivism), while not surprisingly none of the four approaches would consider the habitual reference to socially recognised norms as contestable, yet, all approaches would allow for individual contestation of normativity. The important question, which follows now for the

---

[15] For an excellent example of how to do this with MAXQDA, see Hofius (2014).

theory of contestation, is how the normativity premise may be conceptually integrated in order to fill the legitimacy gap based on equal access to contestation. To do so, it is necessary to turn towards two additional thinking tools.

Transferring these three stages of enacting normative meaning-in-use into the global realm where societal groups, political order and normative rule are neither limited by territorial boundaries, nor bound by the institutional and constitutional settings of a state, adds complexity. This complexity defies the norms conception which is derived from the community ontology standpoint. However, in doing so, it opens up new angles of contestation. After all, as the conceptual *frontier* of normativity is crossed, the likelihood of norm conflict grows. At this point Kant's hospitality principle matters in particular for research on global governance, for it devises the right to cross borders as a right bestowed on citizens as earthlings, not as citizens of nation-states.[16] As globalisation has turned border crossing into a more widely and regularly shared practice in 21st century international relations, the right to visit (albeit not the right to stay, or, for that matter, the right to be welcomed or served) other places has become an important pre-condition for entering into interactions with others. This interaction includes a multitude of different types of actors and extends over the range of policy areas, including foreign policy, defence and security. As Fierke notes, "(O)ver the last century in particular the range of actors involved in some form of cross-border communication related to war has multiplied. Not only states, but international organizations, nongovernmental organizations, journalists, and others have shaped the experience of war" (Fierke 2005: viii).

Whether and if so, under which conditions, these interactions or any international interaction generate conflict, remains to be established by empirical research. The answer is likely to vary. It will depend on a range of contingencies. These inter-national encounters may occur in the context of international organisations, international regimes, in the context of epistemic communities or international conferences, workshops or events where individuals of different national cultural roots encounter each other. They also occur in the environment of multinational corporations. Reversely, it has been shown that with reiterated international encounters transnationalisation reduces the potential for normative conflict, as the distinctiveness of nationally different roots fades, and transnational arenas—therefore—emerge. The following Chap. 3 explores the potential impact of contestation under conditions of diversity in the global realm.

---

[16] See Kant (1984), for a different and somewhat misleading interpretation of the principle see Benhabib (2006), and critically Waldron (2006) in the same volume.

2.4 Conclusion

This chapter explored the normativity premise as the first 'thinking tool' towards a theory of contestation. To that end, it compared four approaches to norms research in international relations (i.e. conventional constructivism, global governance, regime theories and critical constructivism). As the key reference literature for the theory of contestation chapter two revised these approaches, in order to establish first, the allocation of contestable normativity (i.e. as either community-based or practice-generated); second, it identified and compared the analytical approach to norms (i.e. as either structuring, constructed or of dual quality); and third it evaluated the contestability of norms at each of the three distinct stages of norm implementation (i.e. the constituting stage, the referring stage and the implementing stage). Given that at each stage a specific type of agency is predominant, this comparison revealed differences with regard to the expected norm contestability (compare Tables 2.2 and 2.3). While both the constituting and the referring stage show mixed results, all four approaches concur that contestation is expected at the implementing stage. *According to the normativity premise, the implementing stage should therefore be considered as the access point for empirical case studies.*

Chapter 3
The Diversity Premise: The Legitimacy Gap in International Relations

Abstract This chapter focuses on the diversity premise as the second thinking tool. To that end, it draws on diversity claims following empirical accounts of diversity along the ethno-methodological dimension of indexicality, on the one hand, and normative arguments about culturally multiverse constitutional contexts, on the other. It refers to research on governance in the global realm as the terrain where the prospect of establishing and maintaining just and legitimate governance has been considered the greatest challenge and hence been most thoroughly imagined and contested by cosmopolitan philosophers ranging from Kant to Tully. It is argued that Tully's philosophical contestation of Kant's regulative ideal for a political order in Europe on cultural grounds is crucial for the premise of maintaining diversity. The chapter's critical investigation into international relations theories hence applies the diversity premise to challenge the community ontology.

Keywords Diversity premise · Indexicality · Multiverse · Kant · Tully · Legitimacy gap · Normative baggage

Building on the previous chapter's discussion of the normativity premise the following addresses the diversity premise as the second 'thinking tool' towards the theory of contestation. It is argued that the expectation of a high degree of contestation at the implementing stage is not necessarily surprising, given the likelihood that individual agents will consider their own specific preferences prior to deciding in favour of compliance with a global or an international norm. Consider, for example, fishing folks who generally share a sustainable approach to fishing, yet when expected to implement varying fishnet sizes and fishing quotas at specific times of the year, will begin to contest the specific quotas, pointing to their observations of recovering fish stock (e.g. often fishing folk will observe growing fish stock, when governance procedures have just reduced the quotas). This chapter addresses this discrepancy between generally rather high acceptance of fundamental norms such as sustainable fisheries, on the one hand, and highly contested standardised procedures and regulations, on the other. It argues that the emerging 'gap' is not merely coincidental, demonstrating empirical phenomena, but can be conceptually derived as a 'legitimacy gap' in global governance more generally. Following this assumption, it

A. Wiener, *A Theory of Contestation*, SpringerBriefs in Political Science, DOI: 10.1007/978-3-642-55235-9_3, © The Author(s) 2014

is argued that the 'gap' ought to be filled, therefore, by deriving ways of addressing the legitimacy deficit at the referring stage of the norm implementation process. To do that, this chapter applies the 'diversity premise' as the second thinking tool.

Generally, as the previous chapter has demonstrated with the review of the norms literature, it has been noted that both contravening individual interests and a lack of social recognition work against compliant behaviour. That formal validity does not automatically generate social recognition. This is, due to the fact that design of norms (i.e. constitution stage) and compliance with norms (i.e. the implementation stage) are not directly connected. I argue that the 'in-between' step of reference to norms (i.e. the referring stage) provides an empirical access point to explain why this is so, and under which conditions 'design' and 'compliance' might match. The referring stage sheds light on the puzzle that while fundamental norms enjoy wide acceptance both by signatories of international treaties as well as with the wider public, the standardized implementation of these widely accepted norms is contested on the ground on behalf of the designated norm-followers. As noted above, this reference to norms is conceptualised as the practice of re-/ enacting the normative structure of meaning-in-use. While enacting is a social practice, it is interactive rather than purely habitual, and it is reconstitutive rather than cognitive. Shedding light onto the referring stage therefore opens a second empirical access point with regard to the project of assessing the normativity of norms. By doing so, it establishes a conceptual link between the potentially diverse range of individual agents on the one hand, and the changing normative substance of norms, on the other. This practice of 'cultural validation' is therefore considered as the third segment on the cycle of norms (in addition to formal validation and social recognition, compare Table 2.1). Notwithstanding major conceptual advancement in the understanding of the social embeddedness of norms the practice of cultural validation remains under-researched. Therefore this chapter focuses on the diversity premise. The following proceeds in three further sections. Section 3.1 elaborates the argument; Sect. 3.2 introduces the distinction of three—rather than two—distinct norm types; Sect. 3.3 turns to the diversity premise as the second thinking tool of the theory of contestation Sect. 3.4 sheds light on the concept normative baggage Sect. 3.5 addresses the shift from dialogue to mulitlogue.

3.1 Argument: The Legitimacy Gap

At the constituting stage treaty law is purposefully broad-versed so as to be able to include as wide a range of signatories for a document as possible (Chayes and Chayes 1993). Given this emphasis on general agreement, the subsequent contested interpretation of the details of the agreement (whether of legal quality of not) at the implementing stage in specific local contexts is to be expected. Deitelhoff and Zimmermann suggest distinguishing two types of contestation as "justificatory contestation" and "applicatory contestation" (Deitelhoff and Zimmermann 2013, pp. 7–8), which according to the three stages in the norm compliance process would acknowledge possible critical intervention by stakeholders a the constituting and implementing stages, respectively (compare Table 2.1). Both types of contestation reveal the need to develop a more concise analytical understanding of how and where the very normativity of norms is—or ought to be—negotiated in order to obtain and/or maintain fair and legitimate governance in the global realm (see also Müller and Wunderlich 2013). In addition to distinguishing types of contestation, the increasing diversity of the involved agency (including a diversity of types, quality and composition of agency) therefore remains to be addressed. As Zürn, Binder and Ecker-Ehrhardt rightly observe, "the right to justification" (citing Forst 2007) has been demanded by a range of global actors including non-state actors, as well as "formerly less-powerful states against the dominance of strong Western states in international institutions" (Zürn et al. 2012, p. 70). The question of who has access to contestation and how to exercise that right is thus brought into the realm of inter-national relations.

The observation suggests a qualitative shift in global governance theories that take into account the growing diversity of agency. Conceptual advances need to begin by empirically taking 'account of' diversity based on empirical case studies (Wiener 2008; citing Garfinkel 1967; compare also Hofius 2013). The following argues that notwithstanding critical interventions into compliance research and a subsequent growing interest in 'contestation' by critical norm research, the resulting "two level" perception of "norm discourses" (Müller and Wunderlich 2013, p. 9) falls short of the *intermediary level*. Yet, it is here where the *legitimacy gap* in global governance is hidden. To 'uncover' its location and bring its potential for norm research to the fore, I suggest working with a practice-based approach to study inter-national relations as inter-*cultural* relations. To demonstrate how the legitimacy gap may potentially contribute to establish such a platform from which to address contested normativity in international relations, the following section two recalls the distinction of three types of norms and elaborates on the concept of "organising principles" as an intermediary type of norm (Wiener 2008, 2009) with reference to the typology of norms, before turning to the concept of 'multilogue' in the third section.

3.2 Three Types of Norms and the Legitimacy Gap in International Relations

While in principle normative meaning is often agreed, in practice meaning is more likely to be misunderstood. Indicators of this mismatch are provided by situations, in which either the compliance agreement (i.e. the specific norms, rules or regulations that are at stake) is contested by the designated norm-followers (Wiener 2004; Brosig 2012), or where prior commitments (i.e. agreed treaties or conventions) are later called into question (Harmsen 2002). Both international interactive

Table 3.1 Three norm types and the legitimacy gap in international relations

Category	Norms	Moral reach	Degree of contestation
Type 1	Fundamental norms	Broad	Low
Type 2	Organising principles	*Legitimacy Gap*	
Type 3	Standardised procedures	Narrow	High

Source Adaptation from Wiener (2008, p. 66)

law and constructivist norm research have concluded that the formal validity of an agreement does not provide sufficient indication about its implementation. As this section argues, the distinguishing aspect of norms, which would work as an indicator for the degree of normative contestation (and hence the place where normativity needs to be negotiated in order to reflect the diverse experiences and expectations expressed by the multitude of norm addressees, i.e. those who are governed by a norm and expected to comply) is not the fact that a norm is social—for all norms are by definition social, and even the 'legality' of norms requires being demonstrated through practice as Brunnée and Toope have convincingly shown with reference to Fuller (Brunnée and Toope 2010a). What matters instead is the distinct level, where a norm is located on a scale ranging from wide to narrow moral or ethical reach, on the one hand, and low to high degree of contestation, on the other (compare Table 3.1). The following details how and why these three levels matter for the theory of contestation.

Norm research suggests distinguishing three levels for as many types of norms (Wiener 2008, 2009; Wiener and Puetter 2009; Liese 2009; Park and Vetterlein 2010). The levels capture both the diversity of meanings in-use and the diversity of the involved agents. Based on this information multiple actorship and distinct meanings can be related and the level where the highest number of diverse agency is involved should reasonably be the place where normativity stands to be regularly negotiated—whether norms are contested or not. Through *a priori* 'regular contestation' it would thus become possible to pre-empt spontaneous contestation that might turn into conflict afterwards. According to this approach, three norms are distinguished (compare Table 3.1).

Type 1 norms at the meta-level entail universal moral claims that are widely shared, in principle. As fundamental or meta-norms they include both foundational principles of the United Nations community such as, for example, the principle of non-intervention, abstention from torture, human rights or the rule of law (Jackson 2005; Müller and Wunderlich 2013; Liese and Jetschke 2013; Kumm et al. 2013) as well as globally shared norms that are not legally stipulated but taken for granted such as, for example, sustainability or the global commons (Ostrom 1990; Hardin 1968; Scott 2002; Friedman et al. 2005). Given the formal validity as well as the moral weight that is attached to the latter, and which is sustained through the formal framework of treaties, conventions or universal declarations within the framework of international organisations or convents, they are highly likely to be agreed in principle. However, when it comes to implementing these norms 'on the ground' they are most likely to be contested in practice. In turn, *type 2* norms evolve through the very practices of policymaking, jurisprudence or political processes. They are the result of interaction and reflect intersubjective meaning. As organising principles they include, for example the principle of common but differentiated responsibility, the equal culture of sovereignty or the responsibility to protect. For their rootedness in interactive practice they enjoy a more balanced degree of legitimacy in theory *and* in practice, as their moral claims evolve in direct relation with practice.[1] Last not least, *type 3* norms entail specifically defined standards, rules and regulations for specific policy measures.[2] These norms identify specific procedures, which are clearly detailed, for example, by specific provisions of treaties and conventions. They are therefore rarely expected to generate moral issues. However, they are likely to contravene individual interests at the implementation stage.

By distinguishing the morally most broadly defined fundamental norms (such as for example the right to non-intervention, abstention from torture, the rule of law and so on) from organising principles (such as, for example, the responsibility to protect, the culture of sovereign equality or the principle of common but differentiated responsibility) which are generated through politics or policy processes or, for that matter through jurisprudence or jurisgenerative practice, and from standardised procedures (such as stipulated for example by treaties, agreements or conventions) which entail straightforward instructions, it is possible to address specific conditions of compliance, contestation and potential conflict. To demonstrate how this works, Table 3.2 summarizes the sector of security governance and indicates how deliberations at the intermediary level may contribute to fill the legitimacy gap that emerges between fundamental norms of substantially moral quality and, accordingly, a relatively broad scope of generalisation, on the one hand, and standardised procedures of technical quality and a high degree of specialisation, on the other.

What is of prime interest here for the theory of contestation is defining the space where contestation becomes possible, so that conditions for access to contestation can be considered, and subsequently proposals for institutional and/or constitutional change of global governance settings be developed from that vantage point. Once this space is defined theoretically, empirical stages of contestation can be identified. It is argued that, as intermediary level norms, organising principles are conceptualised as the analytical 'space' where normativity becomes negotiable. It is at the point where the intermediary *level* of norms and the *referring stage* of compliance intersect—in politics and/or policy-making—that a conceptual opportunity to establish institutionalised access to regular contestation for multiple stakeholders could be established. In the absence of stable social groups, which would facilitate social recognition that is required to implement international law,

---

[1] Compare Kratochwil and Ruggie's claim about intersubjectivity in regimes, which substantiates this observation (1986).

[2] These norms have also been called "ordinary norms" or "standards" compare, for example, Finnemore and Sikkink (1998), Liese (2006), March and Olsen (1998), Müller and Wunderlich (2013).

Table 3.2 Filling the legitimacy gap in security governance

Category	Norms	Level (Agency)	Example
Type 1: fundamental norms	*Non-intervention* abstention from torture human rights rule of Law Civilian Inviolability	Meta-level (community)	*Type 1* norms are widely shared. They are therefore also considered as global norms such as, for example, the norm of *non-intervention*
Type 2: organising principles	*Responsibility to protect (R2P)* common but differentiated responsibility culture of equal sovereignty	Intermediary level (group)	Legitimacy Gap: *Type 2* norms such as *R2P* are generated within the space indicated by the *legitimacy gap* (i.e. between shared *type 1* and contested *type 3* norms). *Type 2* norms therefore allow for negotiated normativity on a case-by-case basis based on the inclusion of involved stakeholders
Type 3: Standardised Procedures	*Article 2(4) UN Charter* Article 2(7) UN Charter	Micro-level (individual)	*Type 3* norms are contested in inter-national relations. For example: *Article 2(4)* leaves room for different understandings of the non-intervention norm

Source Adaptation from Wiener (2008, p. 66)

the process of negotiating which organising principle might be appropriate, offers to fill the legitimacy gap between shared fundamental norms and contested standardised procedures. In other words, by facilitating the negotiations of the formal validity of fundamental norms with recurrence to the respective cultural experience of the involved actors, cultural validation allows for establishing the lacking sense of appropriateness when social recognition is absent. The following takes this focus on culturally distinct experience that forms each single agent's expectation in inter-national relations up with regard to the diversity premise as the second thinking tool of the theory of contestation. To that end it draws on the diversity debate in public philosophy.[3]

3.3 The Diversity Premise

Substantially, political philosophy offers two distinct approaches to diversity: On the one hand, Kantian regulism, which—for all its merits—is definite and establishes universal principles, and on the other hand, Wittgensteinian pragmatism, which as an agonistic approach, allows for an analytical perspective onto constitutive practices in a constitutional multiverse.[4] While both approaches address the constructive role of 'dialogue' in the process of establishing political order, their respective understanding of the role dialogue plays with regard to cultural diversity differs significantly (Owen 2011). As Tully notes, Habermas expects "that cultural differences would be filtered out in the course of the dialogue, by processes of generalisation and role-taking, and citizens would reach agreement on a difference-blind constitution" (Tully 2008b, p. 41). In turn, the cultural ideal of democratic governance assigns a central constitutive impact of democratic constitutionalism to cultural practice as a constructive dimension of democratic constitutionalism. Thus, Tully emphasises that, "[I]f citizens take into account the culturally different or 'concrete' other, as well as the 'generalized' other, in the course of their deliberation, as they must, then there is no reason in principle why citizens may not be able to give good public reasons for the respect for and public recognition of those differences in diverse forms of constitutions and federations: reasons that are not particular to the members of that culture but are based on considerations of justice, freedom, equality, non-subordination and so on that are shared by citizens generally" (Tully 2008b, pp. 41–42). The practice matters for the principle for it alone reflects the cultural experience which enables the understanding required to follow the moral principles. It works like a cultural footprint to those bothering to look for it. It is the interaction among the

---

[3] Compare Kymlicka (1995), Owen (2011), Tully (2008a, b, 1995, 1993), Tully and Gagnon (2001), Young (1991).

[4] Compare Brandom for this distinction (1998, p. 8, 14; cited in Wiener 2008, p. 205).

participants of a multilogue about shared fundamental norms and principles then, which provides the opportunity to generate shared understandings.

While the public philosophy literature goes much deeper into the conceptual nuances, for the purposes of the theory of contestation, it suffices to summarise that this adds different purposes and possibilities to 'dialogue' in general, and 'contestation' as specific form of critical dialogue with the intention of 'change' by either rejecting the status quo, or making claims towards changing the status quo. To elaborate on contestation as a critical practice, the diversity premise draws on Tully's seminal conceptual insights from studying the phenomenon of "strange multiplicity" within the multi-national Canadian context (Tully 1995). In doing so, it proposes to begin by posing the 'diversity' issue as a central condition, which International Relations theories need to incorporate in a productive manner. For contestations are often ignited by hidden diversity positions. The following elaborates on this proposition. To that end, it recalls the way Tully addresses diversity by raising a simple question, namely, "[C]an a modern constitution recognise and accommodate cultural diversity?" (Tully 1995, p. 1). To answer that question, Tully recovers hidden cultural practices that are constitutive for diversity of the Canadian constitutional frame. In turn, the perspective advanced by this book is interested in respect for diversity as a condition for legitimate and fair governance in the global realm. While the global realm frames an entirely different type of normative order, and the theory of contestation is not aiming to advance a global constitution, the previous two chapters have demonstrated that the international relations literature has encountered contested compliance precisely *because* present diversity conditions of inter-national relations as inter-cultural relations have not been paid sufficient conceptual attention. Accordingly, the diversity premise, as a recurring yet invisible *cause* for contested compliance at the implementing stage, on the one hand, and as the explanation for a *call* for regular contestation at the referring stage, on the other, needs to be explored in more detail.

By addressing diversity upfront, contestation can be conceptualised in a focused way to enhance rather than undermine fair and legitimate governance in the global realm. While this suggestion does not at all aim to discuss diversity within the framework of a global constitution (compare Fassbender 1998, or Habermas 2011 for scholars who apply that frame), it does involve a normative argument about inserting regular contestation at the intermediary level of norms. To that end, I work with a practice approach, which engages the political impact of intercultural diversity in the global realm from the bottom-up (compare Tully 1995; Tully 2002, 2008a, b, as well as Owen 2011). Accordingly, the following elaborates the constitution of normative meaning through a "multilogue of mutual recognition" (Tully 1995, p. 24). It is proposed to adopt the concept of multilogue in order to conceptualise the generation of normativity through the practices of contestation of the diverse stakeholdership that is increasingly common to sectorial governance practices in the global realm (i.e. the sector of fisheries, security, finance, trade, development and so on, compare Krahmann 2010; Park and Vetterlein 2010; Epstein 2012). By linking the diversity premise with the normativity premise it is explored where (i.e. at which of the three stages), normativity is most likely to be contested.

3.4 Normative Baggage

This exploration needs to acknowledge the substance and location of "normative baggage" (Wiener 2007, p. 55), for it provides the source of cultural validation at the implementing stage, and is also malleable and individually held. That is, it only comes to the fore in situations when individual experiences are so clearly opposed that they actually *clash*.[5] The clash situation is relatively likely and therefore requires careful conceptual consideration, because of an important conceptual twist: While normative baggage is not all pervasive, it does travel across borders shouldered by individuals, so to speak. Given this crucial observation regarding the potential impact of normative baggage, it is worthwhile noting that a conceptual distinction exists between the epistemic concept of 'background *knowledge*', which is by definition shared thus generating social recognition of practice understood as competent performance (Adler 2005, p. 21), on the one hand, and the semiotic concept of 'background *experience*' which is individually held and therefore apt to travel across borders is flexible and hence subject to change (Wiener 2008, Chap. 4). It follows that in the absence of social recognition, where nothing seems intuitively appropriate, individuals will turn to their individually held normative baggage for reference. In light of increasing inter-national encounters and the strong likelihood of more rather than less diversity in the world, a better assessment of normative baggage is therefore crucial for understanding the causes of normative conflict and deriving institutional approaches to regulate that conflict potential. It follows that instead of more or better law the legitimacy of governance in the global realm may actually depend on sorting out the normative baggage brought to bear in inter-national encounters because of the legitimacy gap.

To recall, while *conventional* constructivist research on compliance works with the assumption that the disposition to comply with norms is generated by belonging to a group or institution, *critical* constructivism challenges that assumption and explores explanations for and the impact of contested compliance—situated within a specific context. Subsequently, critical constructivists argue that in order to understand contested compliance, other actor constellations

---

[5] For the conceptual background of such 'clash' situations and their particular relevance for bifocal approaches to governance the contributions to the discussion in the context of the Research Project *FISHEU—Contested Norms on the High Seas* funded by the *Volkswagen Foundation* from 2010–2011 at the University of Hamburg and directed by Antje Wiener and Antje Vetterlein were particularly helpful. I would like to thank all participants, especially Chris Shore, Adela Rey, Markus Kornprobst and Antje Vetterlein for their respective comments. Compare, unpublished proceedings of the FISHEU Project, Vienna Workshop held on 25–26 March 2010, on file with author at the University of Hamburg.

and conditions under which contestation occurred needed to be taken into account. The distinction between group-based and individual trajectories of experience and knowledge as indicators for compliance suggests that the more socio-cultural boundaries are crossed, the higher the likelihood of a situation of contested compliance becomes. Given that diverse meanings of fundamental norms are to be expected as being *in use* at all times, our knowledge about normative baggage, including its constitution and use, matters crucially for global governance. While power constellations in international politics will always allow for cutting dialogue short and implementing the norms shared by those in power, this shortcut comes at the cost of legitimacy. This focus on political contestation suggests that by providing the opportunity to question the substantive value of fundamental norms of governance through regular contestation, less powerful agents even though rightful claimants obtain the right to act as stakeholders and, as such have a firm place in the process of re-/negotiating normativity (Owen 2011, p. 134). Tully asks for this potential right to contest and change the rules of the game as the freedom of public philosophers; Fierke has noted this potential with global decision-makers (Fierke 1998); and *the theory of contestation* suggests establishing it as a right for stakeholders of sectorial governance in the global realm.

The subsequent plea for access to contestation is derived from a cultural platform, which conceptualises cultural diversity as a constitutive element of the normative global structure (compare Tully 2008b, esp. Chap. 1). It holds that "[C]onflicting interpretations of norms or contested norm implementation are not necessarily due to a lack of agreement about a norm's meaning. Instead, it may be due to a lack of understanding of that meaning." (Taylor 1993, pp. 47, 50) This insight regarding *agreement* about the inclusion of a specific fundamental norm or principle as part of a constitutive script, on the one hand, and *understanding* the substantive value of that norm with regard to its meaning-in-use from the perspective of diverse agents, on the other, allows for the distinction of several empirical steps. It is therefore of crucial importance for empirical research that seeks to establish, where (i.e. at which of the three stages from norm constitution to norm implementation) to integrate 'nodal points' of contestation in an institutional or, for that matter, a constitutional setting (compare Schwellnus 2006).

3.5 From Dialogue to Multilogue

Notably, the concept of 'multilogue' reflects the notion of place (and therefore the practice of crossing borders) as a source of experience and practical identity. Thus Tully follows Wittgenstein's and Descartes' respective conception of the "map" of a city that has been expanding and developing, street in addition to street and layer upon layer of meaning over centuries (compare Tully 1995, p. 105). By recovering diversity, he seeks to reclaim the terrain upon which "the map of modernity was projected" thereby "hiding the diversity beneath" (Tully 1995, p. 105). The concept of the multilogue summarises the diversity premise well, for it offers an important normative starting point to accommodate diversity in the global realm by maintaining rather than overcoming it. With regard to this book's assessment of the role and resonance of contestation in international relations by way of a critical investigation into International Relations theories, the question arises, *how to account for the normativity generated by multilogues in international relations?* If we define diversity in international relations with reference to, first, the *type of agent* likely to engage in inter-national relations (i.e. including a multiplicity of agents from individuals via social groups to states), and second, with regard to the *type of norm,* which is addressed in specific inter-national encounters (i.e. regarding a specific norm type), we will be able to account for a diversity of normative meanings in-use by drawing on individual background experience and normative baggage. It can be concluded then, that the distinct cultural validation that is advanced through multilogue in these respective contestations reveals the political instances of contestation for cultural cosmopolitanism. That is, it is expected that by making the relation between contested normativity and diversity accessible, normative and institutional (or constitutional) conditions for negotiated normativity be derived. The following Chap. 4 will discuss 'cultural cosmopolitanism' as the third thinking tool for the theory of contestation.

Providing access to contestation for all involved agents—beyond the most powerful and/or legally entitled—would make a difference for a range of global governance decisions, including, for example, enlargement processes of international organisations or regimes. For it would facilitate a procedure to account for and identify different understandings and to develop sustainable agreements. This way, situations prone to backlash such as, for example, when compliance is achieved despite prior disagreement with the rules of others can be avoided. Conceptually, the proposed link between *type 1* and *type 3* norms allows for innovative ways of thinking about solutions to the problem of contested compliance. In order to bridge the gap the proposed turn towards negotiating organizing principles provides a link between the moral claims attached to *type 1* norms on the one hand, and the practical enactment of *type 3* norms, on the other. It establishes a conceptual bridge between the contested universal validity and the constructed socio-cultural quality of norms. In doing so, it highlights the Janus-faced quality of universal claims versus particular expectations towards leading principles of democratic polities in late modernity (Onuf 1994). *Organising principles*—therefore—mark the space where normativity is negotiated by a group and which is constituted by the interrelation between a diversity of agents, arenas and normative meaning-in-use. At the intermediary level normativity is negotiated by a diverse range of agents of global governance. It therefore offers key information about the social construction of legitimacy, which—as international relations theories have shown—is remarkably more important to agents of global governance than legality. The following Chap. 4 will detail the process with regard to establishing the principle of contestedness as a central organising principle for democratic governance in the global realm.

3.6 Conclusion

This chapter has elaborated on the notion of the legitimacy gap and its allocation in the space of everyday politics and policy-making. By doing so, it proposed focusing on the legitimacy *gap*, as an alternative to explaining the democracy *deficit* as an unintended consequence of international institution building, and it suggested for this legitimacy gap to be understood as a theoretical oversight. It was argued that by way of introducing a third level instead of two-level discourses in the norm research literature, a platform for institutional change is created. From this platform access to regular contestation stands to be developed in the following two chapters. In conclusion therefore, this chapter notes that the highest degree of interaction and intersubjectivity is potentially facilitated at the intermediary level where organising principles are contested at the referring stage. This level is therefore considered as the space where *a priori* or routine negotiation about normativity ought to take place. It follows that access to regular contestation would target this space. From this empirical observation about norm types, the following chapter will move on to develop the normative argument about the principle of contestedness. To that end, I take Tully's cultural approach to democratic constitutionalism further towards cultural cosmopolitanism in international relations theories. It is argued that as the third thinking tool 'cultural cosmopolitanism' offers the platform from which to address the legitimacy gap. The following chapter *four* elaborates on the proposal to facilitate a multilogue among stakeholders so as to facilitate the negotiation of normativity under conditions of diversity in global governance.

Chapter 4
Cultural Cosmopolitanism: Contestedness and Contestation

Abstract This chapter introduces the concept of cultural cosmopolitanism as the third thinking tool with a view to framing the theory of contestation. This thinking tool is developed with recourse to Tully's "public philosophy in a new key" (Tully 2008a, b). From this background, the application of this thinking tool towards a critical investigation into international relations theories is aimed to identify the interrelation between the practice of contestation and the principle of contestedness. This is done with reference to the feature of three degrees of contestation (i.e. low, high and regular) in relation with the three types of norms. Understood as a norm-generative practice contestation is considered as a *sine qua non* for legitimacy in any context of governance. It is argued that, in order to make full use of the concept, 'regular' contestation ought to be established as a legitimacy enhancing practice in the global realm. This chapter works with 'cultural cosmopolitanism' as a thinking tool to demonstrate the normative effect of cultural practices in inter-national relations as individual experiences, rather than collective, cultural properties.

Keywords Cultural cosmopolitanism · Public philosophy · Degrees of contestation · Principle of contestedness · Cultural practices · Individual experiences · Cultural validation

This chapter turns to the concept of cultural cosmopolitanism as the third and final thinking tool, which is employed in order to develop a theory of contestation for international relations. In distinction from 'thick' concepts of culture, which assign specific cultural traits and habits to communities (Anderson 1983), cultural cosmopolitanism carries a distinctly 'thin' concept of culture. The concept of cultural cosmopolitanism, which is proposed here considers culture as the sum of background experiences gathered through interactions over time and expressed through the cultural validation of norms in day-to-day life (compare Garfinkel 1967; Geertz 1973; Wenger 1998). This definition of culture is consistent with the practice-approach to inter-national relations insofar, as it takes explicit account of the quality of international relations as inter-cultural relations (compare the diversity premise in Chap. 3). To capture the gap between the shared fundamental norms and the notion of contested compliance with specific rules and standardised procedures, the following suggests that negotiated normativity be conceptualised as a cultural practice.

In critical distinction from the familiar Neo-Kantian reference to political cosmopolitanism, which transports the claim of deontic norm generation through political practice with a view to establishing or changing a specific political order, the concept of cultural cosmopolitanism works with the assumption of cultural practices as having a similarly normative impact on political order. Different from Dahl's well-known 'political contestation' that defines a top-down instrument to measure the degree of liberalisation in democratic regimes (Dahl 1971), the bottom-up concept of cultural practice understands contestation as an expression of respect for the principle of 'mutual recognition' (Taylor 1993; Tully 1995). As such, contestation facilitates the opportunity for stakeholders to participate in negotiating the normativity of governance in the global realm. The following elaborates on the way this distinction matters for the theory of contestation. By doing so, an opening for the participation of involved stakeholders stands to be generated. Three theoretical perspectives distinguish the philosophical origins that matter for allocating the space where regular contestation is to take place in global governance. The *first* stems from liberal democratic theories that advance a top-down perspective to measure democratic quality based on two central indicators to measure the democratic quality of political regimes. They include "public contestation" and the "right to participate"; taken together both indicators are understood as measures to indicate the degrees of liberalisation and inclusiveness of political regimes (Dahl 1971, p. 5; Grande 1996; Merkel and Petring 2012; Neyer 2012). According to this approach, contestation is considered as a *litmus* test of the quality of democratic governance in any given political order. As such, it has become almost a global standard for research on democracy. These theories hold that, as a process, contestation qualifies politics as open-ended and subject to change despite being firmly rooted in the rules of procedure of a particular political order (Rawls 1971). It has been identified as a criterion for setting standards of democratic governance, for example, by Dahl who suggested to consider the "right to access to public contestation" as an indicator for comparative studies on democratic governance (Dahl 1971, p. 4).

By contrast, *secondly*, republican approaches conceptualise contestation as a normatively derived practice, which carries the right to oppose government by contesting the rules, principles and norms of governance from the perspective of the individual citizen. In that case, contestation means maintaining individual freedom vis-à-vis the state. Accordingly, contestation is based on the principle of "contestability" conceived as the right to contest any rule established by the state or government of a given society (Pettit 1997). The republican understanding of contestation therefore indicates the freedom to oppose government rules. In turn, the *third* perspective defines contestation as the freedom to engage with others in dialogue about the norms, principles and rules of governance within a political order. Here, contestation is facilitated by the principle of "mutual recognition", so that access to negotiating the norms and principles of governance on part of the very addressees of these norms is facilitated (Taylor 1993; Tully 1995, 2002;

Tully and Gagnon 2001). According to this approach, contestation is understood as the expression of a political claim to the principle of mutual recognition in culturally diverse contexts of democratic governance. It is therefore employed to assess the democratic quality of political processes based on the claim that "(a) free and democratic society will be legitimate even though its rules of recognition harbour elements of injustice and non-consensus if the citizens are always free to enter into processes of contestation and negotiation of the rules of recognition" (Tully 2000, p. 477). The following elaborates on this bottom-up perspective with reference to 'cultural cosmopolitanism.'

4.1 Cosmopolitanism and Cultural Practice

According to the argument developed above, cultural cosmopolitanism is substantially derived from public philosophy. The definition of cosmopolitanism as 'cultural' builds on two central claims, which have been advanced by bifocal research in public philosophy and International Relations theory: First, cultural cosmopolitanism is considered as a logical extension of the constitutive impact of *cultural practices*, which have been brought to the fore from underneath the regulative map of modernity (Tully 1995). And second, it is a practical consequence of the *cultural validation* of norms as the individual practice of re-/enacting normative meaning-in-use by mobilising socio-cultural background experience at the implementation stage (compare Table 2.3). By highlighting norm-generative impact of cultural practice the concept of 'cultural cosmopolitanism' fleshes out the leading claim of the theory of contestation, namely, that a given community cannot be taken for granted in 21st international relations. Therefore, the legitimacy of fundamental or meta-norms depends on the very conditions under which their normativity is negotiated or morally justified (Geis et al. 2010; Forst 2012; Müller and Wunderlich 2013; Daase and Deitelhoff 2013). In order to explore alternative institutional designs then, these conditions stand to be located, detailed and identified.

The reference to cultural cosmopolitanism (as opposed to the range of adjectives associated with this concept in the history of ideas) is suggested to reflect the diversity premise. It is not proposed with the intention to introduce the kind of 'thick' perception of culture common to communitarian or moral theorists who consider culture exclusively as a collective good (Kleingeld 1999). Instead, cultural cosmopolitanism has been chosen as a thinking tool specifically, in order to transport the impact of cultural practice as expressed in the space of the multilogue. For this multilogue offers a bottom-up approach that enables multiple stakeholders to become involved. It is juxtaposed with Kant's philosophical practice of moral reasoning expressed in the space of a dialogue (Kant 1984). This analytical juxtaposition of two different cosmopolitan logics of practice, which are both constitutive for a particular political order, has been chosen to emphasise the assumption that both are considered as equally important for the constitution of a just political order.

Cultural cosmopolitanism seeks to maintain rather than overcome diversity. Note that this conceptualisation differs from Pauline Kleingeld's description of cultural cosmopolitanism as defining group-based cultural variety. According to Kleingeld's distinction of six varieties of cosmopolitanism, "cultural cosmopolitanism focuses on the value of collectives (cultures), and because it values cultural pluralism positively, cultural cosmopolitanism has some political implications of its own. It implies that states, peoples, and ethnic groups, in their dealings with each other, should value and tolerate cultural differences (provided no basic moral norms are being violated)" (Kleingeld 1999, p. 518). Subsequently, cultural pluralism is considered as a general moral value. By contrast, the point this book seeks to take further is that the roots of global justice may not necessarily be derived from generic claims about morality, but that they draw legitimacy from other than political practices as well. The point is not a claim about morality in general, i.e. implying that "insofar as it is based on the essential moral equality of all human beings, (cultural cosmopolitanism, AW) implies a form of moral cosmopolitanism," (Kleingeld 1999, p. 518). Instead, it is about justice and legitimacy as values that are constituted through everyday practice. Furthermore, the approach to cultural cosmopolitanism in international relations theories advanced by this book does not operate from a generalist position that juxtaposes a collective concept of cultural cosmopolitanism on the one hand, and an individual concept of moral constitutionalism, on the other (Kleingeld 1999, p. 518), and which works with the assumption of 'culture' as the common marker of a moral collectivity.

In sum, following the diversity premise I employ a 'thin' concept of culture, which rests on the key assumption that inter-national relations are to be understood as inter-cultural relations, unless the relatively rare situation of "transnationalisation" can actually be observed (i.e. nationally distinct roots can no longer be identified either with reference to behaviour or with reference to cognition (Wiener 2008, pp. 8, 120)). Notably this understanding of 'culture' works with a constructivist concept as opposed to a primordialist concept of culture (Hale 2004, p. 459). Accordingly, culture is conceptualised as constituted through particular practices, rather than as being given by a societal frame. It follows that instead of working with national differences that are impossible to overcome, this deontic approach to culture stresses that different national roots are indicative for distinct interpretations of norms. Yet, these differences are likely to shrink through iterated interactions. For this contingent understanding of culture based on practice, compare Clifford Geertz's two propositions for an interdisciplinary approach to the study of culture: "The first of these is that culture is best seen not as complexes of concrete behavior patterns—customs, usages, traditions, habit clusters—as has, by and large, been the case up to now, but as a set of control mechanisms—plans, recipes, rules, instructions (what computer engineers call "programs")—for the governing of behavior. The second idea is that man is precisely the animal most desperately dependent upon such extra-genetic, out- side-the-skin control mechanisms, such cultural programs, for ordering his behavior." (Geertz 1973, Chap. 2, p. 44).

Following this perspective, cultural differences are subject to change. And, given the impact of everyday practice on background experience, it follows that in order to account for diverse meanings of norms, it is necessary to reconstruct individual practices of re-/enacting the normative structure of meaning-in-use. Crucially, in the absence of the social environment of a group, which would provide the source of the 'social recognition' and shared appropriateness, the individual practice of cultural validation facilitates the important analytical angle in order to identify the potential contestation of a norm's formal validity. It is argued that in the absence of this sharpened perspective on cultural validation, global norms stand to be potentially contested despite their embeddedness in international treaties, conventions or agreements. To figure out where and how this contestation takes place, the following identifies distinct degrees of contestation with reference to the three types of norms. It is argued that based on this distinction it becomes possible to indicate situations where contestation of shared norms of global governance generates conflict, rather than enhanced legitimacy; and how to counter that process by establishing regular access to contestation. The goal of this distinction is to identify the angle from which 'regular contestation' might be inserted into global governance procedures.

4.2 Modes and Stages of Contestation

This section elaborates on the conceptual link between degrees of contestation and stages of the compliance process. Following the normativity premise, it applies the assumption that both contestation as a political practice (strategic and public questioning of norms, principles or rules of a specific political order) and contestation as a cultural practice (spontaneous disagreement with normative meaning) are constitutive for normative order. For this book's theory of contestation as a concept in international relations theories, the practice of contestation matters in particular with regard to the agreement and implementation of fundamental norms, principles or procedures that are constitutive for the global normative order. In this respect, both implicit and explicit forms of political contestation matter. The implicit practice of contestation includes neglect, negation or disregard. It nourishes discontent and conflict, if it remains unnoticed. It is most likely to generate conflict under crisis conditions, for implicit contestation is likely to eventually come to the fore at unexpected moments, especially under conditions of crisis. In turn, explicit contestation is expressed through the politics of contention including objection, deliberation and/or dissidence (Tarrow et al. 2001). Given that it is always expressed through language, however, it excludes violent acts such as for example any form of war, terrorist acts or protest (for the latter compare Daase and Deitelhoff 2013). What remains to be addressed, therefore is whether or not a distinct type of contestation needs to be considered for the contestation that comes to the fore at the referring stage (compare Table 2.3).

The following addresses this question. To that end it identifies modes of contestation with reference to the three stages of norm implementation in international relations. While recent contributions to constructivist norms research have suggested to rephrase the erstwhile Habermas inspired interactions of 'arguing' and 'bargaining' with reference to types of contestation that are to be distinguished as 'justification' and 'application' related contestation, respectively (compare Deitelhoff and Zimmermann 2013), the *theory of contestation* differentiates according to differences, which are noticeable at a substantively prior level of theorising. Following the critical intervention into international relations theories based on the normativity premise (compare Chap. 2) the core distinction in order to understand diverse effects of contestation is down to two different ontologies around which norms research centres. Thus, an underlying 'community ontology' works with stable normativity claims and therefore does not expect to encounter contestable norms expect at the implementing stage. By contrast, the 'diversity ontology' underlying critical regime theories and critical and consistent constructivism, expects contestable norms at each of the three stages (compare Tables 2.2 and 2.3). The latter ontology allows for distinctive modes of contestation as indicated by the cycle of contestation (compare Fig. 2.1), including for example, modes of moral justification, arbitration, deliberation or contention with regard to the formal validity, the social recognition of norms, or the cultural validation of norms.

The central question that follows from the cycle is less the type but the stage where contestation is possible. Crucially, the community ontology prevents norm contestation at the referring stage. Therefore, the theory of contestation argues that regular contestation needs to be inserted at the intermediary level. It is necessary in order to fill the legitimacy gap between fundamental norms at the meta-level and standardised procedure at the micro-level. As an institutionally warranted practice, regular contestation establishes an enabling procedure that allows 'uncontested' and fair access to negotiate normativity for all stakeholders. In the absence of a conceptual angle that allows for addressing the key problem of lacking social recognition as the central supporting factor towards compliance (compare Finnemore and Toope 2001), only privileged access to contestation is expected at the norm constituting stage, while individual contestation is expected at the implementing stage. As a discursive practice contestation may take a range of specific expressions ranging from discussion, arguing or bargaining via spontaneous or strategic objection to routine deliberation. While contestation always involves dialogue expressed through deliberation, the practice of contestation is contingent with regard to context and involved agency. That is, it is qualified by the environment, in which contestation comes to the fore as a careful deliberation, a routine procedure, or a spontaneous or strategic objection, on the one hand, and by the normative substance, which is distinguished with reference to the three stages of compliance and the three segments that are part of the cycle of contestation, on the other (see Table 2.1). Notably, the subject matter of the moral reach of norms at the constituting stage is most comprehensively addressed by the philosophical literature.

Various traditions of contestation are to be distinguished. For international relations critical theory matters in particular, in both its representations (i.e. as the 'large-C' Critical Theory that is rooted in the theoretical context better known as the Frankfurt School (compare Müller 1994; Deitelhoff and Müller 2005; Diez and Steans 2005), on the one hand, and 'small-c' critical theory which International Relations theorists relate with the Welsh School (Linklater 1998, 2007), on the other. Another practice of critical intervention is represented by the literatures on "feminist contentions" (compare Nicholson 1997; Ackerly 2008), as well as neo-Marxism, Postcolonialism or postmodern theories. All of which evolve around philosophical contestation. The reference to this literature has informed recent norm research on moral justification of fundamental norms at the meta-level (Müller and Wunderlich 2013) in the attempt to identify types of contestation that matter in inter-national relations. Moral justification of normative meaning is derived from the background of philosophical considerations. The practice of questioning the status quo through philosophical contestation is a common practice of critical theories of all stripes. From that background the practice critical public philosophy has advanced a practice-approach to contestation understood as the freedom to change governance principles through pratical phiosophy (Fraser 2005; Forst 2007, 2012; Tully 2008a, b; Owen 2011; Forman and Mackie 2013). As a philosophical practice, contestation means critically engaging with leading assumptions, concepts and theories, and their respective analytical and methodological toolbox.

By contrast, contestation at the implementing stage has been addressed by the compliance literature. It has been addressed in most detail in the context of jurisprudence. As a legal practice contestation means engaging in the routine procedure of juxtaposing legal arguments with reference to the procedure of the law. Given that this practice is much less an intention to question the law, than an intention to keep with the law, it entails the least normatively substantial impact. While the concept had a central role as a routine practice of applying standardised procedures according to specific rules and regulations in jurisprudence, its meaning-in-use in political science is of a different quality and purpose. Contestation in the context of politics or policy-making includes the practices of questioning or even challenging agreements regulations in selected sectors of global governance. This mode of contestation has been observed among others by the development literature (contesting norms of drawing rights, conditions for structural adjustment an so forth), by the fisheries literature (contesting fishing quotas, mesh size, and other regulations), by the environmental literature (contesting emission standards and so forth) or by the security literature (contesting anti-terrorism measures and policy instruments, for example in the UN Security Council). These distinct sector-based contestations involve making claims about political principles, rights and norms vis-à-vis other agents in order to change those norms. They therefore include both collective and individual claims making. Such modes of contestation are a relatively recent phenomenon in international relations. For, so far, the international relations literature—both in law and in politics—has traditionally addressed political contestations either with regard to contested "consent" in the context of international treaty making (Byers 2002, p. 36), or with regard to contested norms in organisational enlargement procedures.[1] It is only recently that contestation has been applied as a means to raise questions about the legitimacy of United Nations decision-making procedures, especially with regard to the UN Security Council, the WTO or the World Bank.[2] Notably, the latter contestation includes the reference to norms, rules or principles, which are considered as generally shared and therefore appropriate by a political majority or by the politically powerful. It is understood as a practice that calls power relations into question—requesting change. The question, which remains to be addressed, is whether the result consists exclusively in a change of a norm or rule itself (i.e. replacing one norm with another), or, whether contestation generates a change of normativity (i.e. changing the very substance of a specific norm that is indicated by the normative structure of meaning-in-use). The former issue has been taken up mostly by the conventional constructivist branch of the human rights literature (Liese 2009); the latter remains to be addressed in more detail. It is at stake here as a central aspect of the theory of contestation.

4.3 Conclusion

Building on the three thinking tools (i.e. the normativity premise, the diversity premise and cultural cosmopolitanism) the theory of contestation suggests operating according to the principle of contestedness as a meta-organising principle at the intermediary level of sectorial governance. The principle of contestedness thus warrants access to regular contestation in processes of renegotiating norms for all affected stakeholders. It is argued that this regular contestation could, for example, be included at say at one of multiple stages in the policy making process. While through reiterated interaction among the same interacting stakeholders regular contestation may also generate a sense of normality and therefore enable the social recognition, to be sure, the theory of contestation argues that as long as international relations operate under the condition of diversity the principle of contestedness remains a central organising principle. Accordingly, it is assumed that, as long as no stable social group environment can be taken for granted, the equality principle maintains that in order to facilitate a generally fair and just procedure, any normative concept must work under the assumption that a community is not in place. The point is that in inter-national relations multiple cultural validations matter not only as an informative and substantial part of the process of political contestation, but also as a multilogical impact on the constitution of political order.

While the normativity premise set the yardstick for reviewing norms research in international relations with reference to the normative roots of leading claims

---

[1] See Brosig (2012), Fierke and Wiener (1999), Wiener and Schwellnus (2004), Wiener (2004), Wiener (2003).

[2] Compare Müller and Wunderlich (2013), Park and Vetterlein (2010), Zürn and Nollkaemper et al. (2012).

raised by the broad ranged compliance literature (compare Chap. 2), the diversity premise set the yardstick for taking the plurality of agency in international relations into account based on their respective individually held socio-cultural experiences (compare Chap. 3). Building on these two thinking tools, this chapter developed 'cultural cosmopolitanism' as the platform from which to approach the specific notion of cultural diversity and the understanding of intercultural dialogue as 'multilogue', which provides a distinct focus onto the multiplicity of stakeholders of global governance.

The previous chapter highlighted the importance of a practice approach to cultural diversity as both indicative of and constitutive for contested normativity. It sought to locate normative contestation with a view to conceptually addressing sites of contestation in inter-national relations. Accordingly, it proposed to facilitate a 'multilogue' among stakeholders of governance so as to facilitate the negotiation of normativity under conditions of diversity in the global realm. Taking up this claim, this chapter argued that, if institutionally established, say in specific sectors of global governance, these sites of contestation could contribute to pre-empt conflict through the insertion of regular contestation at an earlier time in the policy process. Thus regular contestation would be routinely practiced to facilitate a bottom-up participation of multiple stakeholders in order to effectively cap conflict. This proposal rests on the assumption that *the more contestation take place at this level, the higher the chance that misunderstandings or disagreements that are prone to generate conflict through spontaneous or strategic contestation at a later point in time,* are addressed and solved through negotiating normativity at an earlier stage of the compliance process. It is this negotiated normativity, which stands to be explored with reference to the actual place, or indeed, the terrain where the principle of contestedness may be established within any given institutional and or constitutional setting of democratic governance in the global realm. From this platform it is now possible to address the legitimacy gap in international relations through contestation in inter-national relations. The following Chap. 5 will build on this finding.

Chapter 5
Thinking Tools and Central Concepts of the Theory of Contestation

Abstract This chapter proposes that based on the principle of contestedness (as a meta-organising principle of global governance) access to regular contestation at the referring stage ought to be warranted. This stage is sector-specific and therefore requires empirical research for identification. To illustrate this process, this chapter identifies the referring stage with reference to sector-specific organising principles that are derived from processes of policy-making. This application follows the definition of contestation as both indicative and required for legitimacy. Accordingly, the legitimacy gap is indicated by enhanced contestation (i.e. when taken for grantedness and moral value of a norm do not overlap). It is 'space' where normative meanings are contested in IR theories.

Keywords Regular contestation · Sectoral governance · Social recognition · Legitimacy gap · Normative meanings

The following recollects the substantive contribution of three related thinking tools which have been mobilised from public philosophy in order to derive the core concepts of the theory of contestation: first, the normativity premise, second, the diversity premise and third, the concept of cultural cosmopolitanism. These thinking tools were applied to facilitate critical investigations into International Relations theories. Each of these investigations enabled deriving the core assumptions leading towards the theory of contestation for international relations. These include first, the assumption that normativity is created through interaction at three stages of compliance; second, the assumption that normativity is generated through a multilogue and that activates cultural validations; and third, the assumption that regular contestation ought to be inserted at the intermediary level to fill the legitimacy gap, thus bringing the principle of contestedness to bear. The following addresses and recalls these assumptions in their turn.

As the first thinking tool, the *normativity premise* was developed in Chap. 2. As a condition for a theory of contestation it held that normativity must be negotiable, and therefore explored whether and if so which approaches in International Relations theories allowed for negotiated normativity. To that end, it explored the conceptual allocation of the normative roots of norms according to four approaches

A. Wiener, *A Theory of Contestation*, SpringerBriefs in Political Science,
DOI: 10.1007/978-3-642-55235-9_5, © The Author(s) 2014

in IR theories, so as to be able to account for them in practice. With this reference to norms research in international relations it is possible to establish, which of the relevant approaches allow such a potentially problematic concept of contestation. Two criteria of distinction were applied to do this (compare Table 2.1). The *first* criterion raised the question whether an approach located normativity as theoretically 'external' or, reversely, as theoretically 'internal'. The *second* criterion distinguished approaches according to their respective reference to a 'community ontology' or a 'diversity ontology'. The former take the formal validity of a norm as indicative for rule-following, as both Rawls and Habermas would expect, despite their different concepts of justice. The latter considers rules as being constituted through social practices under condition of social patterns or diversity. Based on these criteria chapter two established which approach to norms advanced a *constitutive understanding of normative practice*.

As a result, it was noted that the critical regimes approach and the critical constructivist approach respectively, where most conductive towards allocating configuration about normality, thus offering a practice-based understanding of *negotiated normativity*. In addition two approaches have been singled out: The *first* is the "arguing global governance" approach, which was developed by Bjola and Kornprobst (2011). This approach builds on the deontic theory of John Searle rather than on Kant's "objective catalogue of duties" in order to demonstrate the constitutive power of language, for "Searle's understanding of deontology, by contrast (to Kant, AW), is much broader and thoroughly intersubjectivist" (Bjola and Kornprobst 2011: 11). In doing so, it adds a practice based normative dimension to the constitutive quality of language, which has been developed in particular by consistent constructivist approaches (Fierke 2010). The *second* is the "re-/enacting normative structures of meaning-in-use" approach, which applies the Derridian method of deriving oppositions within a given societal context (Milliken 1999) in order to account for the normative structure of meaning. Again, this approach conceptualises normative meaning as, in principle, subject to change through cultural practice (i.e. everyday practice that validates the meaning of a norm, principle or rule according to experience that forms expectation). It thus allows for a conceptual distinction between cultural validation as an individual practice, on the one hand, and mutual recognition as a social practice, on the other.

The subsequent Chap. 3 developed the *diversity premise* as the second thinking tool. It advanced the assumption that under conditions of globalisation and in the absence of wholesale transnationalisation, inter-national relations must be understood as inter-cultural relations. It concluded that inter-cultural interactions must be considered as the sources of distinct normative claims. Accordingly the diversity premise reflects the impact of cultural validation. Based on the first two thinking tools, it was concluded that, in light of normative meanings, which are subject to change through communication, norm implementation is to be considered as—in principle—problematic. This problematic understanding of norms follows the range of critical norm research in international relations, which demonstrated how and why normative meaning is contingent.

As an intersubjective process, discursive interaction draws on resources, which have been created prior to the negotiating and/or bargaining situation. Communicative action thus not only contributes to the social construction of norms but also reconstructs sociocultural patterns of the life-world. As such, it has a constructive impact both within modern societies and beyond them. If communicative action is conceptualised as intersubjective, it potentially produces "new values" in the process of deliberation (Müller 2001: 173). The challenge for norm research in international relations consisted in addressing the way in which these new values need were actually communicated beyond the relatively close circle of negotiators. For example, in the sector of security governance these would most likely be a group of selected elites. Studying the meaning of norms in a comparative perspective, then, would generate a better understanding about how out-of-context norm interpretation (and conflict) works. In other words, it is suggested that the transfer of normative meanings sheds light on the link between the negotiating actors and their communities of origin. In further elaboration of the theory of contestation, it is argued that by providing access to contestation the conflictive potential of contested meanings can be mobilised for legitimating purposes. This focus on the role of inter-action through language has been addressed widely by the linguistic turn in International Relations theories and in Public Philosophy, respectively.[1] It follows that, unless the normativity premise is considered in relation with the diversity premise, the contingent quality of normativity remains theoretically bracketed. Subsequently, and paradoxically, given that contestation is an *interactive* practice, the mutually constitutive outcome of contestation remains outside the remit of these theories. In sum, the unproblematic conceptualisation of contestation is unable to capture normative change, let alone, to explore contested meanings, which are generated *through* inter-national relations as a set of individual and therefore culturally diverse practices. This shortcoming, in turn, misses constitutive changes *in* International Relations theories. To reverse that paradox, the theory of contestation establishes a platform from which the constitution of normativity in international relations can be addressed.

And Chap. 4 has derived the concept of *cultural cosmopolitanism* from public philosophy as the third thinking tool. Cultural cosmopolitanism summarises the norm-generating force of cultural practices and its impact on the changing norms of political order. It was argued that the concept of cultural cosmopolitanism facilitates address the 'legitimacy gap', which emerges between fundamental norms and standardised procedures at the intermediary level. That is, it works with the assumption of contested normativity and accordingly the demand for access to participation in regular contestation is considered as the meta-norm of global governance, which must be respected in order to establish and maintain legitimate and fair governance in the global realm (Tully and Gagnon 2001), generally

---

[1] Compare work on the Wittgensteinian language game to bear in order to explain or call for 'rule changes' in any type of normative order: See Fierke (1998, 2010, 2013), Onuf (1989, 1994, 2013), as well as Tully (2008a, b).

speaking. How this meta-norm plays out in practice, depends on the institutional procedures and the relevant practices of politics and policy-making within each sector of governance. That is, quite in accordance with the notion that the practice is a "thing and a process" (Onuf 1994) the normative quality of contestation is read off the very interactive practices in these respective sectors of governance (Onuf 1994), on the one hand, while it is normatively negotiated through this practice (Taylor 1993), on the other hand. To establish how the meta-norm of the principle of contestedness plays out in distinct governance sectors in the global realm, empirical research is required. The last section will provide two explorative examples to demonstrate how such research may be operationalized. Prior to that, the following section details the institutional approach to regular contestation with regard to the legitimacy gap in international relations.

5.1 Organising Principles

To conclude the two-tiered argument about the central role organising principles play in filling the legitimacy gap of global governance, this chapter demonstrates how to apply the theory of contestation with reference to selected sectors of global governance. To that end, it begins by recalling the three concepts indicating the place of negotiated normativity, which is indicated by organising principles in global governance according to the theory of contestation. They include, first, the *practice of contestation* indicating the legitimacy gap between publicly shared fundamental norms and highly contested standardised procedures; second, the *principle of contestedness* warranting access to contestation for involved stakeholders, and resulting from the former two, and third, the *policy instrument of regular contestation*, which stands to be facilitated at the referring stage in order to confront the legitimacy gap. All three have been identified through recourse to the three thinking tools, i.e. the normativity premise, the diversity premise and the concept of cultural cosmopolitanism, which have been developed with reference to the social science and public philosophy literatures, respectively. The remainder of the chapter proceeds to allocate the practice of 'regular contestation' on the intermediary level of the norm-type scale, as an option to counter political contestation in politics and policymaking under conditions of inter-national relations.

To fill the legitimacy gap, this section proposes establishing contestedness as a meta-organising principle (i.e. a *type 2* norm) at the intermediary level of governance. Accordingly, it is proposed that International Relations theories conceptualise the legitimacy gap that is indicated by enhanced contestation in a situation, which emerges in most situations when inter-national relations are acted out in the absence of the overlap between formal validity and social recognition of a norm. Subsequently, the legitimacy gap is conceptualised as the 'space' where normative meanings are contested. As it has been argued with reference to the three thinking tools, this is where contestation is to be expected in actual inter-national relations for two reasons. First, according to the normativity premise, normative meaning is re/enacted with reference to distinct normative baggage of the involved actors. Second, according to the diversity premise the encounter of these diverse agents unfolds under the condition of inter-nationality. This interaction is likely to generate of contested normativity, which is enhanced by the legitimacy gap between fundamental norms and standardised procedures. By bringing in the concept of 'cultural cosmopolitanism' as the third thinking tool this legitimacy gap has been conceptualised as the analytical 'space' where meanings stand to be contested. If organising principles are constituted through policymaking and politics, this is where normativity ought to be negotiated. This conceptual framework of the theory of contestation allows for a number of policy options, which will be explored in some detail below. Among them is the suggestion to include a stage in the policymaking and/or political process, where contestation be practiced on a regular basis by all potential stakeholders. By inserting this stage of regular contestation, it is argued, conflictive outcomes as unintended consequences of political contestation can be pre-empted. The legitimacy gap thus matters in particular, for it denotes the space where the cultural diversity of agents (understood as diverse *qua* inter-national distinction) and the diversity of normative meanings-in-use are brought to bear through intersubjective practice (Kratochwil and Ruggie 1986; Kratochwil 1989).

While this is the moment where conflict is expected in the actual politics of inter-national relations, the *theory of contestation* holds that, if implicit or explicit political contestation were to be channelled into regular contestation, conflict could be avoided. By inserting this institutionalised mechanism contestation could target misunderstanding and disagreement and therefore prevent contested compliance from turning into conflict. To demonstrate how this strategic application of contestation is likely to work for the purpose of legitimating fundamental norms in a context where the contestation of meanings is expected *per se* (i.e. notwithstanding the distinction between strategic political contestation or spontaneous habitual contestation), the proposed institutional adaptation of contestedness is explored with regard to three selected sectors of global governance below.

In a subsequent step it is suggested to conceptually locate the legitimacy gap on the *intermediary level* between meta-level norms and micro-level norms. The gap may be allocated in a range of distinct areas of governance including, for example, environmental governance, resource governance or fisheries governance. Compare, for example the norm of sustainability (defined as sustainable use of resources in the global commons), on the one hand, and the rejection of standardised procedures, say emission standards or fishing quotas (defined as standards, regulations and procedures), on the other, which have been agreed in order to implement the appropriate standards through specific policies. The work of norms on the intermediary level will be illustrated with reference to three sectors of governance in section three of this chapter.

Conceptually, the proposed link between fundamental rights (i.e. as *type 1* norms) and standardised procedures (i.e. as *type 3* norms) allows for innovative ways of thinking about solutions to the problem of contestation that has been brought to the fore by instances of contested compliance. In order to fill the gap, it is

Table 5.1 The principle of contestedness and the legitimacy gap

Norm	Contestation	Legitimacy
Type 1	Low contestation	Shared recognition
Type 2	*Regular contestation*	*Legitimacy gap*
Type 3	High contestation	Potential conflict

suggested to turn to organising principles (i.e. the *type 2* norms), which provide a link between the moral claims attached to fundamental norms on the one hand, and the practical enactment of standardised procedures, on the other. It is argued that, while material factors such as resources and power are always a component in the decision to implement rules, social factors such as culture and experience matter for the degree of social appropriateness of a norm as well as the actual individual commitment to implement the relevant rules and regulations. Different from morally grounded fundamental norms and specific standardised procedures, organising principles emerge through contestations in the process of conflictive deliberation about the implementation of fundamental norms such as sustainability, human rights and non-intervention (for a listing of the three distinct norm types). The organising principles that were generated and agreed upon by UN member states through contestations in specific circumstances, such as for example, environmental summits have contributed to define commonly agreed ground rules such as the principles of 'common but differentiated responsibility (CBDR)' or the 'responsibility to protect (R2P).' While remaining contested over the years, to be sure, these ground rules have provided a platform from which to approach future decisions in these respective policy sectors through regular contestation.

Given that organising principles are usually practice-based, that is, they evolve from the "ground up" (Forman and Mackie 2013: 152) through interactive processes of policy-making and politics, they form an important link between fundamental norms and standardised procedures. While standardised procedures are required with a view to implementing specific fundamental norms of a given political order through policy measures or political procedures, they are at the same time, often subject to contention, for they usually constrain the options of the designated norm-followers. Examples where the principle of contestedness would provide a helpful step towards keeping the potential for conflict low include the business sector, which regularly operates on the basis of multinational corporations (Park and Vetterlein 2010) as well as the range of international policies including foreign policy, defence policy, security policy and so forth. With regard to the business sector, consider for example companies such as that regularly include operations in a number of different countries (compare Table 5.1).

As contestation research has shown, inter-national encounters are expected to generate contested interpretations of norms, for the normative structure of meaning-in-use that informs that interpretation and hence the predisposition of whether or not a norm is considered as appropriate, differs according to individual socio-cultural background experience (Wenger 1998; Hofius 2013). In the following three explorative examples are discussed in order to identify such instances of potential conflict and how they can be prevented by 'turning them on their head'

Table 5.2 Reconstructing organising principles of global governance

PART 1: Mapping contestations (macro- and meso-levels)		PART 2: Derive norms (intermediary level)	
Implementing Stage Indicator: Contested *type 3 norms*	*Constituting Stage* Indicator: Contested *type 1 norms*	*Referring Stage* Indicator of shared legitimacy	*Filling the Legitimacy Gap?* Answer: Research question
Map: Contestations of *type 3 norms*	Reconstruct: Contestations of *type 1 norms*	Reconstruct: Emergence of *type 2 norms* (organising principles)	Compare: *Type 2 norms* in selected governance sectors

Source Adapted from Wiener et al. (2012)

(i.e. by adding regular contestation as an additional step in the policy process of a given governance sector). The examples of contested norms of governance include the sector of climate governance and the sector of security governance. Each situation will be addressed in their turn below. In practice, the following sketches how an empirical research design could benefit from the theory of contestation (compare Table 5.2) with regard to research operationalisation in order to conduct empirical research.

To shed light on the legitimacy gap as the space where contestation is expected the empirical research is operationalized within two broader parts. *Part one* includes the selection of cases in specific governance sectors, such as, for example fisheries governance, security governance, environmental governance and so forth. And *Part two* includes the process of deriving norms at the intermediary level. The two parts include four distinct empirical steps (compare Table 5.2). Step one consists of mapping contested meanings of fundamental norms at the meta-level, step two reconstructs organising principles which are generated through international inter-actions, step three compares these organising principles over time and with reference to different cases, and step four derives the organising principles at the intermediary level. More in detail empirical research is likely to focus on a range of case studies in the selected policy sector and involves discourse analytical methods applied to interview data and policy documents in combination with ethnographic approaches such as participant observation.

This empirical research should include interviews and observation of processes of norm interpretation and implementation in conjunction with knowledge production and translation within and between policy communities, inter/national bureaucratic settings as well as academia and non-state advocacy groups such as non-governmental organisations. The case studies will then reconstruct the resulting organising principle with reference to the process of negotiating normativity and based on the knowledge within and across the cases' respective arenas. The focus of these case studies will be set on background experiences that inform the way normative meaning-in-use is re-/enacted with regard to the leading fundamental norm of a specific governance sector. The term 'sector' rather than 'epistemic community' has been chosen to reflect the diversity—as opposed to commonality—which sets the conditions of compliance in most sectors of global—as opposed to local or national—governance. Through this reconstruction of the cultural validation of normative meaning it becomes possible to identify contested meanings. This allows for inductive conclusions about organising principles constituted through interaction, which matter for each case, and which stands to be compared *within* governance sectors. Finally, empirical research stands to link the findings and transfer them back to the global governance literature to conclude with an interactive account of governance in the global realm.

Chapter 6
Applying the Theory of Contestation: Three Sectors of Global Governance

Abstract To illustrate the potential value-added of the theory of contestation for research on global governance, this chapter turns to three explorative cases in which the relation between types of norms is presented through sector-specific narratives. The cases and the respective selection of norms that play a role at the three stages of norm implementation include security governance (e.g. civilian inviolability, responsibility to protect, non-intervention), climate governance (e.g. sustainability, common but differentiated responsibility, emissions standards) and fisheries governance (e.g. sustainable fisheries, precautionary principle, fishing quotas).

Keywords Climate governance · Security governance · Fisheries governance · Types of norms · Stages of norm implementation · Organising principles · Compliance

To demonstrate how empirical research programmes might address and examine potential organising principles, the following explores their role in three selected policy sectors. In keeping with the bifocal approach two steps are to be reflected by research that seeks to analyse the legitimacy gap. The first step consists of identifying organising principles in a selected sector of global governance, and the second step assesses how to 'fill' the legitimacy gap through regular contestation. The crucial aspect of this bifocal approach lies in linking the normative meta-organising principle of contestedness with the practice of contestation, which is required in order to establish the location of the legitimacy gap. That is, specific sector related organising principles are derived through reconstructive empirical research. This practice-based approach is required in order to generate the necessary data, which are required for reconstructing organising principles on the ground, so to speak. Thus it becomes possible to reflect and understand the contingency of background experiences of the involved stakeholders. After all, it is this background experience that informs the cultural validation as one of the three elements in the cycle of norm contestation. Organising principles that have become acknowledged as legitimate norms are therefore more likely to be accepted by stakeholders than standardised procedures. In turn, as norms that have been socially constructed through ongoing re-enactment of the normative structure of meaning-in-use, organising principles

A. Wiener, *A Theory of Contestation*, SpringerBriefs in Political Science,
DOI: 10.1007/978-3-642-55235-9_6, © The Author(s) 2014

are most likely to have become routinized, compare, for example the principle of common but differentiated responsibility (R2P). As such they have accumulated normative substance that is shared by a number of stakeholders. Following this reconstruction of organising principles as *type 2* norms at the intermediary level, the second step addresses potential problems with access to regular contestation with regard to the group of involved stakeholders and so on.

Whether the identified organising principles suffice to actually fill a specific legitimacy gap stands to be established by subsequent larger-scale empirical research. The following explores this approach with reference to three selected governance sectors. In each of these, specific organising principles can be derived through reconstructive analysis. Thus, in the sector of *security governance* the most well known organising principle is the responsibility to protect (R2P), in the sector of *climate governance* the organising principles include the—older—principle common but differentiated responsibility (CBDR) as well as the more recently developed principle of equitable access to sustainable development (EASD), and in the sector of *fisheries governance* the organising principles include the ecosystem approach next to the precautionary principle and the equity principle.[1] Given the limited scope of this publication each sector and the respective organising principles are briefly introduced with reference to the sectors own specific narrative, while the place for thorough and systematic comparison is elsewhere.[2] Accordingly, the following turns to the three selected governance sectors in order to demonstrate how regular contestation 'works' as a practice that is conducive towards generating organising principles as the outcome of negotiated normativity, and how this practice might be sensibly introduced in order to enhance the quality of just and legitimate governance in international relations.

6.1 Organising Principles of Security, Climate and Fisheries Governance

This section turns to three explorative case studies in order to demonstrate how the theory of contestation might be used in applied research. It details the examples of contested compliance that result from the legitimacy gap between fundamental

---

[1] According to the Canadian governance, the approach is define thus: "An **ecosystem approach** requires that fisheries management decisions consider the impact of the fishery not only on the target species, but also on non-target species, seafloor habitats, and the ecosystems of which these species are a part. This approach also requires that management decisions take into account changes in the ecosystem, which may affect the species being fished. This includes the effects of weather and climate, and the interactions of target fish stocks with predators, competitors, and prey species." Emphasis in original text, for details, sees: http://www.dfo-mpo.gc.ca/fm-gp/peches-fisheries/fish-ren-peche/sff-cpd/ecosys-back-fiche-eng.htm; (accessed 14 March 2014).

[2] These sectoral comparisons are going to be undertaken within the framework of another project.

Table 6.1 Organizing principles in selected sectors of global governance

Governance sector/levels	Climate	Security	Fisheries
Meta	Sustainability	Non-intervention, sovereignty, civilian inviolability	Sustainable fisheries
Intermediary	CBDR/EASD	R2P	Ecosystem approach; equity principle; precautionary principle
Micro	Emission standards etc.	UN charter articles, regulations, etc.	Fishing quotas, mesh-size, etc.

norms and standardized procedures in the sectors of security, climate and fisheries governance respectively (compare Table 6.1).

All these are governance sectors of international relations, which have been widely researched.[3] In each of them principles, such as for example of common but differentiated responsibility, the responsibility to protect, or the equity principle are relatively well known to the research community as well as to politicians and other research users. However, so far, the literature has not related to them as organising principles. Instead, especially the responsibility to protect, and recently, the principle of common but differentiated responsibility have been at the centre of discussions about their quality with regard to their forward validity (whether legal or not) and about their appropriateness (were they fair and up to-date). However, some authors did notice the importance of the "gap" and the contestation revolving from the tension between fundamental norms on the one hand, and the rules and regulations to implement them, on the other (see especially Bernstein 2009). While the result of communicative processes among involved stakeholders, these principles have so far not been understood as generated through the interactive process of contestation.

Yet, as the theory of contestation argues, the very contestations that are observable in these sectors could be established so as to facilitate 'regular' contestation. This would then – according to the principle of contestedness – be accessible to all involved stakeholders. This could, for example, be established as an institutionalized measure to warrant purposeful contestation at specific stages of the policy process. In other words, according to the theory of contestation these organising principles are expected to reflect negotiated normativity. I therefore suggest that they be valued as governance norms with often considerably more weight than fundamental norms which have been included in international law, but which are often less respected by the increasingly diverse group of inter-national agency. The following demonstrates the emergence of organising principles with reference to three selected governance sectors.

---

[3] See for example Bernstein (2009), Bernstein and Pauly (2007), Falkner (2013), Hochstetler and Viola (2012), Jentoft (2007), Jessel (2010), Krahmann (2007, 2011), Ørebech (2013).

6.2 Organising Principles in Three Governance Sectors

6.2.1 Security Governance

As one of the traditional core policies of international relations (understood as inter-state politics) the sector of security governance is most explicitly organised with reference to fundamental norms at the meta-level. These are stipulated by international law and generally accepted, albeit not necessarily uncontested by the designated norm-followers, i.e. the United Nations' member states. The leading paradox with regard to fundamental norms in the sector of security governance, i.e. the affirmation of the principles of non-intervention and sovereignty through 'contested compliance' with these very norms, has most notably come to the fore in the process of the decision about the military intervention into Iraq. For it shed light on a series of contestations about those very norms. This contestation demonstrates well how, despite the broad appreciation of these meta-norms, and despite the repeated affirmation of that very appreciation through multilateral treaty agreements and conventions, their contestation has become the rule rather than the exception in the sector of security governance. The ongoing and rather controversial disputes about decisions to enforce the principle of civilian inviolability through humanitarian intervention have demonstrated these contestations most clearly. Subsequently, it can be summarised that despite of widely shared fundamental norms in security policy, including first and foremost the fundamental principle of sovereign equality for United Nations member states that is sustained by the principle of non-intervention, these fundamental norms are often threatened precisely for the reason of their frequently contested implementation involving a diversity of agents and therefore a significant variation of individual background experiences. Here, national or community interests interfere with expectations towards the uncontested implementation of required procedures according to various United Nations Charter articles, such as, for example, Article 2(4) which specifies the abstention from the threat of force, and Article 2(7) which details the principle of non-intervention, respectively.[4]

Prior to the Iraq related contestations, discussions about the moral obligation to protect human rights unfolded with regard to the atrocities in Rwanda and Srebenica and the related debates about the duty to intervene applying the use of force, including the military interventions in Afghanistan and Kosovo. They also

---

[4] That "(A)ll members shall refrain in their international relations from the threat or use of force against the territorial or political independence of any state; or in any other manner inconsistent with the purposes of the United Nations." And, that "(N)othing contained in the present Charter shall authorise the United Nations to intervene in matters which are essentially within the domestic jurisdiction of any state or shall require the members to submit such matters to settlement under the present Charter; but this principle shall not prejudice the application of enforcement measures under Chapter VII." See: UN Charter Articles 2(4) and 2(7), respectively, at: http://www.un.org/en/documents/charter/chapter1.shtml (accessed 14 March 2014).

involved contestations about the implementation of the two fundamental norms of abstention from the use of force and non-intervention. Two propositions emerged from these deliberations: first, the responsibility to protect (R2P) which was established by the International Commission on Intervention and State Sovereignty (ICISS) in 2001[5]; and second, the principle of civilian inviolability, which was proposed by legal scholars (Slaughter and Burke-White 2002).

It has been convincingly demonstrated, especially with the rising power of the BRICS, that multilateralism has largely and increasingly failed (Hochstetler 2012).[6] Are meta-norms of security governance therefore generally to be considered as weak? According to the theory of contestation this must not necessarily be the case. The theory of contestation holds that the ultimate goal regarding norm compliance in global governance is not about obtaining *legality* (i.e. establishing the distinctive quality of a norm) but about *legitimacy* (i.e. establishing the normative quality of a practice). While interactive international law seeks to establish whether a norm, such as for example the responsibility to protect, has transgressed into a "legal" norm, or whether it is still an "emerging" norm (Toope 2000), and therefore considers legality as the distinctive criterion, the theory of contestation aims to establish 'legitimacy' through regular contestation. As Kornprobst notes in this regard, "I define public justification as a communicative process through which a political community converges on what it regards as compelling reasons upon which to act" (Kornprobst 2012, p. 5; see also Müller and Wunderlich 2013). According to the theory of contestation it is precisely these interactions and their capacity to reflect distinct cultural validations, which are constitutive for organising principles which matter. For they allow the diverse group of inter-national agents with a stake in the decision to assume stakeholdership through their partaking in the space where normativity is negotiated. While, pending on the specific conditions of interaction e.g. according to frequency and actor constellation, this interactive process does also bear the potential for group formation. However this occurs actively if and when transnational arenas emerge under circumstances of reiterated interaction. This has been observed, for example in the context of stable international organisations such as the European Union or the United Nations.

Given the likelihood of this result, the goal of the theory of contestation is not necessarily the emergence of a group-based social recognition. While social groups are likely to emerge following reiterated interactions in all sectors of global

---

[5] For details, see the ICISS report titled 'The Responsibility to Protect' (2001); see: http://www. icj-cij.org/homepage (accessed on 14 March 2014); see also, for many contributions on the emergence and standing of this norm Sands (2006) and Gholiagha (2014, forthcoming).

[6] For discussions about the decline of multilateralism as an indicator of contested top-down norm implementation vis-à-vis new forms of coordinated multilateralism that indicate new practices of bottom-up strategies of compliance, I am indebted to Kathryn Hochstetler. I benefited hugely from her expertise on global governance during our "Schanzen Conversations" when she was a Visiting Professor at the German Institute for Global Area Studies in Hamburg throughout November 2013.

governance, and social learning will kick in, the *theory of contestation* holds that given the condition of diversity despite globalisation, the impact of social group formation is not expected to solve the problem of contested compliance. It will therefore be treated as an exception, albeit one that does require attention as an enhancing factor towards norm acceptance. In turn, access to negotiated normativity based on the principle of contestedness is expected to facilitate the opportunity to create stakeholdership through regular contestation as an institutionalised procedure. While Brunnée and Toope's scrutiny of a decade's contested implementation of the responsibility to protect finds that the principle largely fails, for it is not a legal norm, yet noting "that, if there is no congruence between norm and action, no practice of legality, we will have to conclude that the responsibility to protect has not yet emerged as a legal norm" (Brunnée and Toope 2010b, p. 209), others have shown that—even the most powerful United Nations member states—go to quite some length in order to legitimate their action, whether in accordance with international law or not. This comes as no surprise to critical norms research that would expect enhanced contestation in situations where social recognition cannot be expected in inter-national negotiations. As Fierke notes, it is the analysis that focuses on the various "background conditions that made a forceful intervention possible in, for instance, Kosovo or Afghanistan, rather than an analysis of the use of force itself. Any particular act of interference *is constituted* or made possible *by a larger set of assumptions, rules and practices*" (Fierke 2005, pp. viii–ix). That is, it matters now these context conditions are negotiated. And, according to the respective normativity and diversity premises it is therefore important to establish who has access to these negotiations that are prior to and constitutive for the interpretation of the compliance conditions, under which decisions about humanitarian interventions are ultimately taken.

6.2.2 Climate Governance

Like in most governance sectors the trajectory of politics and policy making of climate governance includes committee meetings, draft procedures, *ad hoc* meetings and so on, which take place in the context of international organisations and their related institutional settings. All of these document processes of deliberation and—pending on the circumstances—contestation about the three types of norms, including organising principles. These processes include drafting formal documents such as conventions, treaties and agreements as well as generating informal resources such as memorandums, minutes and routinised procedures (Scott and Trubek 2002). Given that the *theory of contestation* builds on approaches that apply the 'diversity ontology', the term 'sector' rather than 'regime' or 'epistemic community' has been chosen. Thus I pre-empt assumptions about pre-existing communities as contexts of norm implementation, unless their existence is empirically derived. In the sector of climate governance the implementation of specific regulations to generate and support the general sustainability norm, such as the well-known emission standards is among the most prominent regulatory measures (Bernstein 2009, 2013; Hochstetler and Viola 2012; Hochstetler 2012; Falkner 2013).

According to the literature their implementation depends on, first, the commitment of governments to sign international conventions and agreements (i.e. the constituting stage) and second, the interests of multiple agents at the bottom of the compliance chain (i.e. the implementing stage). While the development of norms in the sector of climate governance had taken a turn that raised hopes among their supporters in the early 1990s, current developments are less optimistic. Thus, it is interesting to note how the concept of common but differentiated responsibilities (CBDR) which was established in the 1992 UN Framework Convention on Climate Change (UNFCCC).[7] The CBDR principle has developed "increasing recognition in international law" (Stone 2004, p. 276; Harris 1999) and, as such become an organising principle in so far as it allowed for subsequent meetings which brought actors in the climate sector together under the umbrella norm of sustainability, to avoid discussions to establish whether or not responsibility towards sustainable climate preservation was an issue in the first place. In other words, responsibility was taken for granted by all stakeholders. In addition the CBDR principle entails the recognition of diverse responsibilities of the involved actors. While the matter of how to interpret 'differentiation' remained an issue, the duty to engage in climate preserving issues was set nonetheless. As a principle that has brought negotiators to the global table, the CBDR principle has therefore become an important organising principle. It "involves three key features. First, it establishes the common responsibility of all States to protect the environment of the earth. Second, it requires states to pay "in accordance with their [...] differentiated responsibilities [...] [because] the largest share of historical and current global emissions of greenhouse gases has originated in developed countries". Third, it requires states to pay "in accordance with [...] their respective capabilities" (Hedahl 2013, p. 1, citing the UNFCCC).

While over the past two decades it's pulling power has declined, CBDR thus presented "one of the normative starting points" of climate governance (Hochstetler 2012, p. 963), and therefore a "cornerstone of sustainable development" (De Lucia 2012). More recently, the UNFCCC has called for the principle of "equitable access to sustainable development" which is seen as a way to insert more attention towards the moral justification of sustainability. Whether this principle holds and turns into an organizing principle with equal pulling power as the CBDR principle remains to be seen and documented with reference to the coming decade of climate governance. A change in the compliance process has been marked by increasingly coordinated efforts of the group of countries called

---

[7] The UN Framework Convention on Climate Change took place in New York in 1992, for further information see the Report on the Workshop of Equitable Access to Sustainable Development of the Ad Hoc Working Group on Long-term Cooperative Action, published by the UN, New York, Framework Convention on Climate Change, 2012, see also: https://unfccc.int/essential_background/items/6031.php, (accessed 14 March 2014).

BASICs[8] who while agreeing that CBDR was conducive towards a change in the quality of commitments to comply with norms in the climate sector, now seek to pursue climate policy implementations, which are crafted from their own, national, perspectives and under their own respective responsibilities. Over the past decade this has led to a shift from the top-down quality of multilaterally agreed meta-norms towards a bottom-up quality of "unilateral quality" in as much as compliance with climate norms depends increasingly on voluntary commitments to comply, which is expressed by single countries vis-à-vis specific regulations (Hochstetler 2012, p. 961). In this case, the reference to organising principles and monitoring their emergence, role and resonance over time, provides an important reference for a better understanding of such strategic policy changes as well as the shift from one organising principle to another. In fact, a higher appreciation of CBDR as an organising principle would allow more room for manoeuver concerning single country preferences with regard to specific demands at the implementing stage. What matters, is that the stakeholders' views are respected at the referring stage (compare Table 2.3). This is likely to become the central focus for future research on the role and resonance of the principle of equitable access to sustainable development.

6.2.3 Fisheries Governance

Like any other sector of governance the sector of fisheries governance involves the setting of principles, regulations and procedures.[9] In this sector the implementation of specific regulations such as fishing quotas or the limit of mesh-size reduction are considered as particularly rational, for they are not only reasonable but also scientifically recommended measures against over-fishing, so that the remaining life-stock can recover in the mid- to long-term. While the point has been demonstrated and commented upon in numerous academic publications with reference to sound scientific, economic and social science data, the following highlights a case that illustrates why data alone fail to convince the designated nonfollowers. To that end, it turns to the so-called 'turbot war' between Canada and Spain in the mid-1990s as an example to demonstrate the necessity of a solid and systematic approach to fill the legitimacy gap between meta-norms and standardised procedures in the sector of fisheries governance.[10] In the 1990s, what has been called

---

[8] The BASICs include the four large developing countries of Brazil, South Africa, India and China, which formed by an agreement on 28 November 2009.

[9] For the concept of "fisheries governance" within the United Nations institutional setting, compare the website of the Fisheries and Aquaculture Department of the Food and Agricultural Organisation (FAO) at: http://www.fao.org/fishery/topic/2014/en; (accessed 14 March 2014).

[10] The 'turbot war' lasted from 9 March to 16 April 1995, involving Canada, the UK and the EU. For references to the 'turbot war' see, for example, Howe and Kerby (2009), Joyner and Alvarez (1996), see also Cornago (2010).

"the collapse of the Grand Bank cod fisheries" has brought a serious reduction of Greenland turbot stock. The collapse resulted in significant job losses in the Canadian Atlantic fisheries, leaving about 50,000 unemployed.[11] "By the 1990s, the Newfoundland cod fishery had collapsed, forcing the government to declare a moratorium on all fishing" (Vogt 2010).[12] That is, in order to counter the imminent fish stock extinction the Canadian Government decided to implement a zero quota for Atlantic cod fisheries of Nova Scotia. Accordingly, it was prohibited to fish for cod within the 200 NM Economic Exclusive Zone (EEZ) off the Canadian Atlantic coast. The decision caused massive protest among the Canadian fishing folk who contested the legitimacy of that quota for two reasons. The first reason was subject to domestic contention, for a zero quota meant that their livelihood was threatened. After all it meant going out of work without the offer of an alternative employment programme. The second reason of contesting the decision at the implementing stage was that foreign vessels continued to fish the grounds right beyond the EEZ, where the fish was breeding. In this context, the fact that, five years later in 1995, the *Estai* a Galician vessel from Spain fished turbot just off the 200 miles zone in international waters, using a mesh-size that did not comply with the legal norm, meant a major provocation of sorts. The Canadians protested against the fact that "other countries were also targeting the Greenland turbot, often fishing right *on the edge* of Canada's Exclusive Economic Zone (EEZ) and using fishing gear which was illegal under Canadian law, such as small-mesh nets. The Canadians also claimed that foreign vessels had quotas that were set too high, fished too intensively and their overfishing on the edge of the EEZ was going to undo all the conservation measures that Canada had put in place to restore their fish stocks."[13] The situation subsequently led to massive contestation, involving even the use of martial means, when the Canadian Navy in collaboration with the Coast Guard and the fishing trawlers on location, seized the Galician trawler in order to demonstrate the breach with their fisheries governance norm, using gunfire in the process (Schaefer 1995/96, p. 437). The *Estai* was captured, their fishing net taken to the UN headquarters in New York by Brian Tobin, then Canada's Fisheries Secretary, to demonstrate the Spaniard's breach with the mesh-size regulation.

What happened here, and what does the situation demonstrate with regard to the problem of the legitimacy gap? There have been many different accounts of this event including different descriptions of the involved parties, for example, the *Estai* has been interchangeably identified as Spanish, Galician, European and so

---

[11] For details on the Grand Bank fisheries, see: http://britishseafishing.co.uk/the-collapse-of-the-grand-banks-cod-fishery/ (accessed 14 March 2014).

[12] See: http://www.humanities360.com/index.php/brian-tobin-and-the-turbot-war-of-1995-19910/ on p. 1 (accessed: 19 March 2014).

[13] For the source of this report, see: http://britishseafishing.co.uk/the-turbot-war/ (accessed 14 March 2014). (Emphasis added AW).

on. While much can be said about this, the point here is to demonstrate how different segments in the cycle of contestation come into play (compare Fig. 2.1). While the regulations set by the Canadian authorities were reasonable in order to sustain the recovery of fish-stock and thereby the livelihood of the fishing folks in the long run, they had a dramatic and immediate effect on that very livelihood there and then. In turn, the Galician vessel's conduct of fishing turbot was legal according to their understanding of fishing in international waters where no mesh-size regulations for turbot were in place at the time.[14] That is, their behaviour was in accordance with the regulations set by the Northwest Atlantic Fisheries Organisation (NAFO).[15] After all, the Spanish trawler kept fishing outside the EEZ and was therefore outside Canadian sovereign territory.

However, the scenario was perceived altogether differently by the involved Canadians: In their perception the *Estai* challenged the norms of fisheries governance in two ways: First, by using mesh-size that was cut smaller than Canadian regulations established (Matthews 1996, p. 514) their behaviour contested the formal validity of Canadian mesh-size regulations. Notably, however, the international NAFO regulations did not formally establish any mesh-size regulations and could therefore, not be breached by the Spaniards. Second, by this perceived over-fishing of turbot at a time when Canadian fishing folk had faced unemployment and misery following the zero quota decision on Atlantic cod five years earlier, the Canadian cultural validation of the Spaniards' behaviour enhanced the perception of the Spaniards' wrong-doing. As a result, the Canadians who sought to protect the fish-stock felt their attack of the Spanish trawler, while formally illegal, was legitimate both with regard to the sustainability principle (i.e. the fundamental norm of sustainable fisheries) in protection of the global commons, and with regard to their perceived right to protect their livelihood based on their respective background experience.[16]

---

[14] As Tobin claimed in the Canadian House of Commons: "(T)he net had a 115 mm mesh, which is smaller than the 130 mm required by NAFO. In addition, the net in question had an 80 mm liner in the net. (Commons Debates, 15 March 1995, p. 10511)" (cited in Matthews 1996, p. 514).

[15] As an intergovernmental fisheries science and management body, "NAFO was founded in 1979 as a successor to International Commission of the Northwest Atlantic Fisheries (ICNAF) (1949–1978). NAFO's overall objective is to contribute through consultation and cooperation to the optimum utilization, rational management and conservation of the fishery resources of the NAFO Convention Area. The NAFO **Convention** on Future Multilateral Cooperation in the Northwest Atlantic Fisheries applies to most fishery resources of the Northwest Atlantic except salmon, tunas/marlins, whales, and sedentary species (e.g. shellfish). Currently NAFO has 12 Members from North America, Europe, Asia and the Caribbean. Among them are four coastal states bordering the Convention Area: USA, Canada, France (in respect of St. Pierre et Miquelon), and Denmark (in respect of Faroe Islands and Greenland)." For details see: http://www.nafo.int (accessed 14 March 2014).

[16] According to Matthews, the Canadian action was justified with reference "to moral rather than legal terms" (Matthews 1996, p. 505).

This situation demonstrates the cross-purposes of legality and legitimacy quite well: While the Canadian moratorium sought to preserve one type of fish stock (cod), the fact that other fish (turbot), which was caught by using means that were in breach with their specific mesh-size regulations, the incident demonstrates the often stark contradiction between what is perceived as right and therefore legitimate by the involved stakeholders. As the *theory of contestation* holds, this difference in perception matters. It is due to the diversity of experience and expectation of the involved stakeholders. While all might agree on the fundamental necessity to protect the global commons through commitments, the diversity principle is likely to contravene that agreement, i.e. by deviating from the norm at the implementing stage. This narrative of an escalation of contested norms into an inter-national conflict demonstrates that the practices of extending fishing zones and managing fishing quotas have always been linked with the politics and the culture of the respective society of their origin. In recent decades the extinction of fish-stock has become a real possibility and, subsequently, fisheries policy has become an issue of security and survival on a global scale. In sum, the incident illustrates the importance of reference to the three norm types in order to explain contested compliance and to prevent conflict. It entails two major contestations: First, the mesh-size norm for Atlantic turbot fishing was not implemented by the Spanish trawler *Estai* (*type 3* norm), and second, the international norm of non-intervention was not implemented by the Canadian navy when firing their guns at the *Estai* in order to obtain that net (*type 1* norm). In addition, it resulted in an agreement to establish joint quotas and a new more rigorous control regime based on mutual recognition with reference to the North Atlantic Fisheries Organisation (NAFO) (*type 2* norm).[17]

The *theory of contestation* holds that countering the global challenge of the extinction of fish stock is not exclusively a matter of implementation. Instead it involves the deeper and more complex issues of shared validation of fisheries regulations by *all* involved stakeholders, despite the absence of social recognition in the global commons as that context, to which implementation of the fundamental norm of sustainability refers. Following norms research in international relations theories, it can be argued that successful implementation of fishing quotas (and especially, the plethora of detailed regulations, policies and norms that are required to implement the quotas) depends on enhanced legitimacy through interactive processes and on contextualised policy making reflecting economic, cultural and societal conditions of fisheries policy. Therefore the involvement of the range of stakeholders in handling the problem of contested compliance with fisheries norms may have generated a different approach that respected mutual interests and diverse perspectives. In other cases, regional fishing councils have generated regulations that were conducive towards successful fish stock recoveries. Compare for example, the case of Norwegian and Russian collaboration

---

[17] For detailed notes regarding the outcome, see: House of Commons, *Hansard Debates*, 18 April 1995, Column 20; emphasis added AW; http://www.publications.parliament.uk/pa/cm199495/cmhansrd/1995-04-18/Debate-1.html (accessed: 19 March 2014).

towards the preservation of cod in the Northern Sea (Ørebech 2013) or the successful preservation of cod in the North Sea and the Baltic Sea through stakeholder involvement at the referring stage (Jessel 2010).[18] Whether or not the precautionary principle, the equity principle or others principles are appropriate organising principles remains to be demonstrated with reference to further empirical research.

6.3 Conclusion: Contestation at the Referring Stage

This chapter sought to provide a perspective on the value-added of the theory of contestation with regard to studies on compliance in selected sectors of global governance. It first briefly recalled the three thinking tools which had been mobilised with reference to social science theories and public philosophy (i.e. the normativity premise, the diversity premise and the concept of cultural cosmopolitanism) in order to conduct critical investigations into International Relations theories, and then addressed the problem of contested compliance with global norms that were long believed to be steady, solid and widely respected. It then identified the core elements of the theory of contestation, namely, negotiated normativity, regular contestation, and the principle of contestedness. From this framework, the third section addressed three exploratory cases in which the theory of contestation was applied in order to illustrate processes of contested compliance and the emergence of organising principles through interactive negotiations around the implementation of meta-norms in the governance sectors of security, climate and fisheries respectively.

In sum, the insight provided into three different narratives of routinely emerging organising principles (i.e. R2P, CBDR as well as the precautionary principle), suggest that normative framework conditions matter considerably for compliance with norms. Clearly, they constitute different possibilities and constraints in the three sectors. Their different impact on the task of 'filling the legitimacy gap' at the intermediary level is reconstructed thus with reference to the three stages of compliance. First, at the constituting stage of the process of norm implementation the concepts of civilian inviolability, non-intervention, abstention from the use of force as well as sustainability are considered as widely recognised fundamental norms at the meta-level. Each norm bears reference to moral ideas about all

---

[18] Compare, for example, the case of cod fisheries in Russia and Norway, or the case of cod fisheries in the North Sea and in the Baltic Sea, see Jessel (2010), pp. 73–85. For further information about the Russian–Norwegian Maritime Boundary Dispute, see: FISHEU—Contested Norms of Fisheries Governance, research project, directed by Prof. Dr. Antje Wiener and Dr. Antje Vetterlein, founded in 2010 at the University of Hamburg, details at: http://www.wiso.uni-hamburg.de/professuren/global-governance/forschung/kuerzlich-fertiggestellte-projekte/fisheu (accessed 14 March 2014); see also Hønneland (2011).

humankind and the protection of the individual's right to remain unharmed. As such, they entail claims to protect and maintain the global commons and the individual as the guardian and benefactor of that commons, implying the social and economic long-term viability of human industrial activity and resource use.[19] According to the typology of norms (compare Table 3.1) it can be summarised that with regard to these fundamental norms a low degree of contestation is expected, for their moral sway is widely accepted in principle. The respective framework convention or charter reflect this wide acceptance among UN member states, compare, for example, references in the United Nations Convention of the Law of the Sea; the United Nations Framework Convention on Climate Change; or the Human Rights Charter of the United Nations. As the examples demonstrate, by contrast, at the implementing stage, the perception of standardised procedures and specific regulations is much more likely to be contested.

Therefore the legitimacy gap at the referring stage needs to be addressed and the point of regular contestation for all involved stakeholders comes in. How regular contestation is to be institutionalised needs to be addressed on the basis of large-scale evaluative and comparative case studies (for a research template to operationalize these, compare Table 6.2). The *theory of contestation* holds that strategically established instances of regular contestation would allow a multiplicity of actors to claim the right to get involved.[20] In the process, re/enacting normative meaning-in-use would improve the conditions for compromise. This would, in turn, sustain the implementation of quite detailed limitations about fishing quotas, the size of mesh, emission standards including emission trading as well as a range of detailed specifications of minority rights, human rights or individual rights are often highly contested at the implementation stage by the designated norm-followers.

As the *theory of contestation* has argued, these explicit or implicit contestations could be countered by 'filling the legitimacy gap' at the referring stage, i.e. between meta-level and micro-level norms through the insertion of regular contestation. By doing so a meta-organising principle of contestedness would be brought to bear by way of establishing access to regular contestation and thereby the opportunity to reflect the experience held by the involved stakeholders, the potential for conflict were expected to decline. For example, research on norm implementation in selected sectors of governance would begin by examining

---

[19] Compare Forman and Mackie (2013), Kratochwil (2014), Ostrom (1990), Rawls (2002), Sen (2009) Slaughter (2005), Ruggie (2005).

[20] While this book has worked with a human-centric concept of contestation throughout, i.e. assuming that the right of access to regular contestation be claimed and put into practice by human beings, there are other concepts of actorship such as, for example, ecosystems as well as 'Gaia', who also hold legitimate claims to stakeholdership. I thank Jim Tully for this observation. While it brings the "Gaia hypothesis" to the fore, (Tully 1995), the argument leading beyond human-centric contestation is particularly important in the fields of ecology, earth science and climate science. Space limitations do not allow for an in-depth discussion of this argument in this book, however.

Table 6.2 Empirical research setting

Level of analysis	Norm type	Method/data/source	Main questions	Operationalisation
Regulatory and normative	Fundamental norms	Text analysis—documents	Change of norms over time/regional differences	Underlying paradigms/ knowledge/theories
Policy	Organising principles	Policy analysis— documents/ interviews	Changing policies and justifications/distribution of Interests/positions of relevant stakeholders (States, NGOs etc.)	Justifications/frames
Experience	Standardized procedures	Interviews and observation	Compliance/non-compliance/negotiations of norms	Practices

Source (Wiener and Vetterlein 2011)

situations of contested norms with regard to the three stages of compliance. Based on this material, it then becomes possible to identify the involved agents, establish the conditions for stakeholders' access to contestation, and accordingly assess the given opportunities for stakeholders to engage in establishing the ground rules that are agreeable to the involved stakeholders (or, at least an acceptable majority of that group) in order to establish the conditions for norm implementation.

Such case studies do not necessarily need to start from scratch, but would in the best case scenario begin with successful instances of norm implementation in a selected governance sector (compare Table 6.2). For example, case studies would first look at successful instances of negotiated normativity through coordination among selected stakeholders (as demonstrated by the emerging countries in the climate sector, or by regional fisheries councils in the fisheries sector). This sequence reflects the need to compare the setting of negotiated normativity in successful cases with instances in which a selected policy towards implementing the details following constitutive treaties or framework conventions failed to deliver. This comparison stands to demonstrate empirically, whether, how and where, the task of filling the legitimacy gap between meta-norms and standardized procedures can be addressed with reference to emerging through organizing principles at the intermediary level empirically and access to regular contestation.

Chapter 7
Conclusion: Why a New Theory of Contestation?

Abstract This chapter summarises the book's objective to develop the theory of contestation by highlighting the interrelation between contestation as a norm-generative practice and contestedness as a meta-organising principle of global governance. It highlights the central claim that by understanding contestation as a critical discursive practice that is constitutive for normative change, a constructive contribution is made to the legitimacy 'deficit' debate. That is, it facilitates ways to allocate and establish regular contestation in selected sectors of governance, based on this innovative approach to theorising legitimate and just governance in the global realm under conditions of ongoing globalisation and inter-nationality.

Keywords Contestation · Contestedness · Legitimacy deficit · Legitimacy gap · Inter-nationality · Meta-organising principle

This book developed the theory of contestation in order to generate an enhanced conceptual understanding of the legitimacy gap in global governance, and, relatedly, identify potential ways of addressing the gap in practice. The theory entails four main features. They include (1) a typology of norms, (2) distinct modes of contestation, (3) stages of norm implementation and (4) segments on the cycle of norm validation. It was motivated by two observations: First, references to 'contestation' have become abundant in work on international relations throughout the social sciences, philosophy and law, yet the meaning of the concept appears to become less specific the more it was used. Second, the issue of contested legitimacy despite widely shared formal validity of fundamental norms as well as the accompanying rules of procedure and regulations on the ground, has become a pressing problem, especially, when cross-border issues of global governance in the global realm are at stake. However, it is these cross-border issues such as security governance, climate governance, oceans governance, water governance among others that form a central aspect of today's international relations. And while the global commons has been regulated with reference to human kind as its constituent power, the absence of interactive ways of handling the norms that preserve that heritage has meant that it is now increasingly under duress. The theory of contestation is presented as an interactive inter-national way of addressing that problem of global governance.

To that end, the *theory of contestation* suggests working with the concept of legitimacy 'gap' as opposed to the legitimacy 'deficit' which has been more commonly used in global governance theories. This distinction has been made in order to unbind the concept of legitimacy from the inevitable reference to state-bound concepts of legitimacy such as, for example, principal-agent theory, or theories of global justice (compare for many Rawls 2002; Pogge 2009). To develop the theory of contestation as a bifocal approach I have derived thinking tools form public philosophy that reflects normative claims and understands contestation as a norm-generative practice, derive from public philosophy thinking tools. Based on these, a series of critical investigations into international relations theories have been conducted in order to address the legitimacy gap.

Conceptually speaking, this gap was localised on the intermediary level in between widely shared fundamental norms with broad moral and ethical reach on the one hand, and often highly contested standardised procedures with clear instruction for compliance, on the other. The need for a 'theory' that takes up the concept of contestation emerged from the increasingly wide application of the concept, which was paralleled by a growing lack of specification of the concept's substance; hence the concern that it's cutting edge might get lost as a result. To revive that erstwhile critical potential and make it available to systematic critical and empirical research in international relations the *theory of contestation* undertook three related methodological steps: *Step one* identified three 'thinking tools' that were derived from public philosophy so as to substantiate the core elements of a theory of contestation from the larger context of normative theories (compare Chaps. 2–4). *Step two* used these thinking tools to undertake critical investigations into International Relations theories in order to identify research assumptions as to the application of 'contestation' research in international relations (compare Chap. 5). And *step three* explored how these research assumptions could be best applied with a view to mapping global governance sectors in order to derive organising principles (i.e. *type 2* norms) at the intermediary level. By doing so it was intended to fill the gap between widely accepted fundamental norms (*type 1*) at the meta-level, on the one hand, and highly contested micro-norms (*type 3*) at the micro-level, on the other (compare Chap. 6).

This final chapter summarises the value-added of the theory of contestation. The thinking tools have been applied to conduct critical investigations into international relations theories, and especially, the relevant contributions to norm research as offered by conventional and critical constructivism, regime theories and global governance. The resulting theory of contestation reflects the leading principles of public philosophy insofar as it critically applies basic normative philosophical concepts in practice. Based on this interdisciplinary background and the bifocal approach it becomes possible to study international relations as a field where inter-national relations are understood as inter-cultural relations. Thus it sets new standards of legitimate and fair governance in the global realm under conditions of globalisation and pluralism. From that background, the theory of contestation was presented as a bottom-up alternative to norm research that places norms within a community ontology. Accordingly, it was argued that while the concept of community has been studied widely, having become under-estimated by those who stick to the structuring power of anarchy on the one hand, and over-estimated by those who emphasise the structuring power of communities of practice, on the other the norm-generative quality of inter-national relations remained underexplored. To uncover this norm-generative quality the *theory of contestation* is intended as the first port of call, for scholars interested in applying insights from public philosophy in real world international relations. It therefore has been dubbed something akin to a manual on 'contestation.' In concluding, the book's main points are summarised below. To that end, the following first turns to the selection of thinking tools and the respective research assumptions, and then focuses on organising principles as ground rules of global governance, which are to be derived through access to regular contestation by the involved stakeholders.

7.1 Thinking Tools and Research Assumptions

The book introduced three thinking tools from public philosophy, namely the normativity premise, the diversity premise and the concept of cultural cosmopolitanism. The theory of contestation centres on the interplay between the contestation (as a discursive practice) and contestedness (as the normative 'ground rule' for just and legitimate governance) in the global realm. Both were derived from applying these thinking tools towards a critical investigation into International Relations theories. Subsequently, it was first argued that the legitimacy deficit in global governance should be conceptualised as a legitimacy gap. This was demonstrated by identifying the legitimacy gap as the space where norms are most likely to be contested in the process of norm implementation. Building on this insight it was, secondly, argued that allocating the gap makes it possible to address the stage of norm compliance where normativity is most likely to be contested, i.e. at the intermediary level where norm clashes become predictable. For it is here where not only normative acceptance and personal interests often clash on a vertical axis, but where also inter-national diversity is most likely to play out on a horizontal axis. Accordingly, it is here, where the legitimacy needs to be constituted through stakeholder interaction. It was suggested that at that stage norms should therefore be regularly negotiated by involved stakeholders. Thus conflictive political contestation could be pre-empted by access to regular contestation by all involved stakeholders. The latter stand to be established as an institutionalised or, under specific circumstances such as, for example, the European Union, also based on quasi-constitutionalised procedures.

Over the past six chapters, the book engaged in critical investigations into International Relations. In doing so, it followed the tradition of placing International Relations theories within the broader context of the Social Sciences and Public Philosophy. Picking up the long-standing question which triggered the norm research programme and kept it alive for three decades, of how norms 'work' (Kratochwil 1984), it was argued that in order to answer that question, International Relations theories required a more refined understanding of cultural practices as norm-generative. And, by drawing on public philosophy, it was held that norms research in International Relations theories stands to benefit from extending their understanding of political cosmopolitanism towards one of 'cultural cosmopolitanism.'

7.2 Organising Principles and Regular Contestation

To demonstrate how the theoretical argument might be used in subsequent empirical research it was illustrated with reference to selected sectors of governance, that the intermediary level between fundamental norms (i.e. *type 1* norms) and standardised procedures (i.e. *type 3* norms) left a legitimacy gap as the terrain where the institutionalisation of access to regular contestation would offer a viable alternative towards establishing just and legitimate governance in the global realm while preserving a pluralist setting of global politics. By focusing on the constitutive power of practices as norm-generative, and by taking into account the premises of normativity and diversity, *the theory of contestation* offers a contribution to International Relations theories insofar as it addressed the legitimacy gap in order to fill it (as opposed to bridging it!). As such, the theory of contestation offers an important conceptual tool to grasp conflict situations that are likely to occur in the fields of international organisations, regime theory and transnational law. In addition, the bifocal perspective on the legitimacy gap allows for the conceptualisation of regular contestation as a practice that is constitutive for just and legitimate governance based on the principle of contestedness. To that end, it provided an explorative application of the theory with regard to identifying organising principles in three sectors of governance by deriving them reconstructively. Based on the explorative cases of climate governance, security governance and fisheries governance, it derived the organising principles of common but differentiated responsibility, the responsibility to protect, equity, and the precautionary principles, respectively, as principles that have been developed through ongoing contestations at the intermediary level. Thus, it was argued, the legitimacy gap between the fundamental norms, which had been established at the constituting stage, on the one hand, and the standardised procedures and regulations, which had been highly contested at the implementing stage on the other, were negotiated in a series of contestations at the referring stage. The resulting claim of the theory of contestation is to reflexively approach these insights with reference to the meta-organising principle of contestedness and to allocate institutionally warranted access to contestation.

7.3 Conclusion

Generally, and with regard to further international relations theories, the *theory of contestation* carries a turn towards normative theorising in international relations. For it raises a question about who has access to contestation under specific conditions. Given that contestation is not merely a habitual reaction to norms and rules, which are taken for granted but stems from critical reflection *about* norms, the concept is more encompassing than the concepts of bargaining and arguing, which it has effectively come to replace. It involves identifying normative principles and in order to identify these, a question about the social group that establishes the rules of access to critical dialogue about the rules that govern the group needs to be raised. While contestation is the task of the involved lawyers in a legal case, access to contestation is not given, but must be established by 'the rules of the game' in social or political environments with reference to certain regulations or principles. As an interactive process, contestation is conducive towards establishing the terms of legitimacy in the interaction between norm-setters and designated norm-followers. Therefore as a critical practice in international relations contestation means questioning the very principles of governance. As such, the concept is promising with a view to counter legitimacy problems of governance in the global realm. To tease out this potential, this book proceeded with critical investigations into international relations in order to scrutinise the use of the concept of contestation in International Relations theories. The research was motivated by the observation of the declining conceptual 'teeth' of contestation. To counter that development it worked with the reminder from democratic theory that as long access to contestation is not warranted everyone affected by a norm, the legitimacy problem persists. The theory of contestation responds to this problem by mapping the complex field of contestation in inter-national relations, and by arguing that the practice of contestation itself has the capacity to establish warranted access to regular contestation.

References

Ackerly, B. (2008). Feminist methodological reflection. In A. Klotz & D. Prakash (Eds.), *Qualitative methods in international relations: A pluralist guide* (pp. 28–42). Hampshire: Palgrave Macmillan.

Adler, E. (2005). *Communitarian international relations: The epistemic foundations of international relations*. London and New York: Routledge.

Adler, E., & Pouliot, V. (Eds.). (2011). *International practices*. Cambridge: Cambridge University Press.

Albert, M. (2003). Entgrenzung und Internationale Beziehungen: Der doppelte Strukturwandel eines Gegenstandes und seines Faches. In G. Hellmann, K. D. Wolf & M. Zürn (Eds.), *Die neuen Internationalen Beziehungen. Forschungsstand und Perspektiven in Deutschland* (pp. 555–576). Baden-Baden: Nomos Verlagsgesellschaft.

Anderson, B. (1983). *Imagined communities*. London: Verso.

Benford, R. D. (2011). Framing global governance from below: discursive opportunities and challenges in the transnational social movement arena. In C. Bjola & M. Kornprobst (Eds.), *Arguing global governance. agency, lifeworld, and shared reasoning* (pp. 67-84). Oxford: Routledge.

Benhabib, S. (2006). *Another cosmopolitanism*. Oxford: Oxford University Press.

Benhabib, S. (2007). Twilight of sovereignty or the emergence of cosmopolitan norms? Rethinking citizenship in volatile times. *Citizenship Studies, 11*(1), 19–36.

Benhabib, S., Butler, J., Cornell, D., & Fraser, N. (1995). *Feminist contentions: A philosophical exchange*. London and New York: Routledge.

Bernstein, S. (2009). Conclusion. In S. Bernstein & W. D. Coleman (Eds.), *Unsettled legitimacy. political community, power, and authority in a global era* (pp. 317–330). Vancouver: University of British Columbia Press.

Bernstein, S. (2013). Global environmental norms. In R. Falkner (Ed.), *The handbook of global climate and environment policy* (pp. 127–145). Oxford: Wiley-Blackwell.

Bernstein, S., & Pauly, L. W. (Eds.). (2007). *Global liberalism and political order: Toward a new grand compromise?*. Albany: State University of New York Press.

Bially Mattern, J. (2011). A practice theory of emotions for international relations. In E. Adler & V. Pouliot (Eds.), *International practices* (pp. 63–86). Cambridge: Cambridge University Press.

Bjola, C., & Kornprobst, M. (Eds.). (2011). *Arguing global governance. Agency, lifeworld and shared reasoning*. Oxford: Routledge.

Bjola, C., & Kornprobst, M. (2013). *Understanding international diplomacy: Theory, practice and ethics*. London: Routledge.

Börzel, T. A., & Risse, T. (2000). When Europe hits home: Europeanization and domestic change. *European Integration Online Papers (EIoP), 4*(15), 1–24.

Brandom, R. B. (1998). *Making it explicit. Reasoning, representing, and discursive commitment*. Cambridge, MA: Harvard University Press.

Brosig, M. (2012). No space for constructivism? A critical appraisal of European compliance research. *Perspectives on European Politics and Society, 13*(4), 390–407.

Brown, C. (1992). *International relations theory: New normative approaches.* New York: Harvester Wheatsheaf.

Brown, C., & Ainley, K. (2005). *Understanding international relations.* Basingstoke: Palgrave Macmillan.

Brunnée, J., & Toope, S. J. (2010a). *Legitimacy and legality in international law: An interactional account.* Cambridge: Cambridge University Press.

Brunnée, J., & Toope, S. J. (2010b). The responsibility to protect and the use of force: Building legality? *Global Responsibility to Protect, 2*(3), 191–212.

Buchanan, A., & Keohane, R. O. (2006). The legitimacy of global governance institutions. *Ethics and International Affairs, 20*(4), 405–437.

Burchill, S., Linklater, A., Devetak, R., Donnelly, J., Nardin, T., Paterson, M., et al. (Eds.). (2009). *Theories of international relations.* Hampshire: Palgrave Macmillan.

Byers, M. (2002). The shifting foundations of international law: A decade of forceful measures against Iraq. *European Journal of International Law, 13*(1), 21–41.

Carlsnaes, W., Risse, T., & Simmons, B. A. (Eds.). (2002). *Handbook of international relations.* London: Sage.

Chayes, A., & Chayes, A. H. (1993). On compliance. *International Organization, 47*(2), 175–205.

Checkel, J. T. (1998). The constructivist turn in international relations theory. *World Politics, 50*(2), 324–348.

Checkel, J. T. (2000). *Building new identities*? Debating Fundamental Rights in European Institutions, ARENA Working Papers 00(12), Universitetet i Oslo, Oslo.

Checkel, J. T. (2001). Why comply? Social learning and European identity change. *International Organization, 55*(3), 553–588.

Christiansen, T., Jørgensen, K. E., & Wiener, A. (1999). The social construction of Europe. *Journal of European Public Policy, 6*(4), 528–544.

Clark, A. M., Friedman, E. J., & Hochstetler, K. (1999). Sovereignty, Global Civil Society, and the Social Conferences: NGOS and States at the UN Conferences on Population, Social Development, and Human Settlements. *Conference Paper. 40th Annual Convention of the International Studies Association.* Washington, 16–20 February 1999.

Cochran, M. (1999). *Normative theory in international relations: A pragmatic approach.* Cambridge: Cambridge University Press.

Cohen, J. L. (2012). *Globalization and sovereignty: Rethinking legality, legitimacy, and constitutionalism.* Cambridge: Cambridge University Press.

Cornago, N. (2010). *FISHEU: Contest Norms on the High Seas. Workshop Paper.* Planning Workshop: FISHEU-Contested Norms of Fisheries Governance. Hamburg, 22–23 January 2010.

Cox, R. W. (1983). Gramsci hegemony and international relations: An essay in method. *Millennium, 12*(2), 162–177.

Daase, C., & Deitelhoff, N. (2013). Internationale Dissidenz - ein Forschungsprogramm. In J. Junk & C. Volk (Eds.), *Macht und Widerstand in der globalen Politik* (pp. 163–175). Baden-Baden: Nomos.

Dahl, R. A. (1971). *Poliarchy: Participation and opposition.* New Haven: Yale University Press.

De Búrca, G. (2009). The EU, the European court of justice and the international legal order after Kadi. *Harvard International Law Journal, 51*(1), 1–49.

De Búrca, G., & Weiler, J. H. H. (Eds.). (2012). *The worlds of European constitutionalism.* Cambridge: Cambridge University Press.

De Lucia, V. (2012). Common but differentiated responsibility, environmental law and policy. *The encyclopedia of Earth.* Retrieved March 14, 2014, from http://www.eoearth.org/view/article/151320/.

Deitelhoff, N. (2009). The discursive process of legalization: Charting Islands of persuasion in the ICC case. *International Organization, 63*(1), 33–65.

Deitelhoff, N., & Müller, H. (2005). Theoretical paradise—empirically lost? Arguing with Habermas. *Review of International Studies, 31*(1), 167–179.

Deitelhoff, N., & Zimmermann, L. (2013). *Things we lost in the fire: How different types of contestation affect the validity of international norms.* Paper prepared for presentation at the International Studies Association Convention, Toronto, 26–29 March 2014, pp. 28.

Diez, T., Bode, I., & Fernandes da Costa, A. (Eds.). (2011). *Key concepts in international relations.* London: Sage.

Diez, T., & Steans, J. (2005). A useful dialogue? Habermas and international relations. *Review of International Studies, 31*(1), 127–140.

Doty, R. L. (1993). Foreign policy as social construction: A post-positivist analysis of U.S. counterinsurgency policy in the Philippines. *International Studies Quarterly, 37*(3), 297–320.

Dunne, T., Kurki, M., & Smith, S. (Eds.). (2010). *International relations theories: Discipline and diversity.* Oxford: Oxford University Press.

Dunoff, J. L., & Pollack, M. A. (Eds.). (2013). *Interdisciplinary perspectives on international law and international relations: The state of art.* Cambridge: Cambridge University Press.

Duvall, R., & Chowdhury, A. (2011). Practices of theory. In E. Adler & V. Pouliot (Eds.), *International practices* (pp. 335–354). Cambridge: Cambridge University Press.

Engle Merry, S. (2011). Measuring the world indicators, human rights, and global governance. *Current Anthrolopogy, 52*(3), 83–95.

Epstein, C. (2012). Stop telling us how to behave: socialization or infantilization? *International Studies Perspectives, 13*(2), 135–145.

Erskine, T. (2013). Normative international relations theory. In T. Dunne, M. Kurki & S. Smith (Eds.), *International relations theory: discipline and diversity* (pp. 36-58). Oxford: Oxford University Press.

Falkner, R. (Ed.). (2013). *The handbook of global climate and environment policy.* Oxford: Wiley-Blackwell.

Fassbender, B. (1998). *UN security council reform and the right to veto. A constitutional perspective.* The Hague: Kluwer Law International.

Fierke, K. M. (1998). *Changing games, changing strategies.* Manchester: Manchester University Press.

Fierke, K. M. (2005). *Diplomatic interventions—conflict and change in a globalizing world.* Hampshire: Palgrave.

Fierke, K. M. (2010). Constructivism. In T. Dunne, M. Kurki & S. Smith (Eds.), *International relations theory: discipline and diversity* (177–194). Oxford: Oxford University Press.

Fierke, K. M. (2013). *Political self-sacrifice: Agency, body and emotion in international relations.* Cambridge: Cambridge University Press.

Fierke, K. M., & Jørgensen, K. E. (Eds.). (2001). *Constructing international relations: The next generation.* Armonk, NY: M.E. Sharpe.

Fierke, K. M., & Wiener, A. (1999). Constructing institutional interests: EU and NATO enlargement. *Journal of European Public Policy, 6*(5), 721–742.

Finnemore, M. (1996). *National interests in international society.* Ithaca: Cornell University Press.

Finnemore, M. (2000). Are legal norms distinctive? *Journal of International Law and Politics, 32*(3), 699–705.

Finnemore, M., & Sikkink, K. (1998). International norm dynamics and political change. *International Organization, 52*(4), 887–917.

Finnemore, M., & Toope, S. J. (2001). Alternatives to 'legalization': Richer views of law and politics. *International Organization, 55*(3), 743–758.

Forman, F., & Mackie, G. (2013). Introduction: New frontiers in global justice. *Critical Review of International Social and Political Philosophy, 16*(2), 151–161.

Forst, R. (2007). *Das Recht auf Rechtfertigung.* Frankfurt/Main: Suhrkamp.

Forst, R. (2012). *The right to justification. elements of a constructivist theory of justice*. New York: Columbia University Press.

Fraser, N. (2005). Reframing justice in a globalizing world. *New Left Review 36*, 69–88 (Nov–Dec 2005).

Friedman, E. J., Hochstetler, K., & Clark, A. M. (Eds.). (2005). *Sovereignty, Democracy, and Global Civil Society. State-Society Relations at UN World Conferences*. New York: State University of New York Press.

Fuller, L. L. (1969). *The morality of law* (rev ed.). New Haven: Yale University Press.

Gallie, W. B. (1956). Proceedings of the Aristotelian Society. Conference Paper. Meeting of the Aristotelian Society. London, 12 March 1956, pp. 167–198.

Garfinkel, H. (1967). *Studies in ethnomethodology*. Cambridge: Polity Press.

Geertz, C. (1973). *The interpretation of cultures: Selected essays*. New York: Basic Books.

Geis, A., Müller, H., & Schörnig, N. (2010). Liberale Demokratien und Krieg: Warum Manche Kämpfen und Andere Nicht. *Zeitschrift für Internationale Beziehungen, 17*(2), 171–202.

Gholiagha, S. (2014). The responsibility to protect: Words, deeds and humanitarian interventions. *Journal of International Political Theory, 10*(3), 361–370 (Review Essay).

Giddens, A. (1979). *Central problems in social theory*. Berkeley: University of California Press.

Grande, E. (1996). Demokratische Legitimation und Europäische Integration. *Leviathan, 24*(3), 339–360.

Habermas, J. (1988a). *Theorie des Kommunikativen Handelns. Handlungsrationalität und Gesellschaftliche Rationalisierung*. Frankfurt/M: Suhrkamp.

Habermas, J. (1988b). *Theorie des Kommunikativen Handelns. Zur Kritik der Funktionalistischen Vernunft*. Frankfurt/M: Suhrkamp.

Habermas, J. (1991). Citizenship and national identity: Some reflections on the future of Europe. *Praxis International, 12*(1), 1–19.

Habermas, J. (2011). *Zur Verfassung Europas. Ein Essay*. Frankfurt am Main: Suhrkamp Verlag.

Hale, H. (2004). Explaining ethnicity. *Comparative Political Studies, 37*(4), 458–485.

Hanagan, M. (1999). Introduction: changing citizenship, changing states. In M. Hanagan & C. Tilly (Eds.), *Extending citizenship, reconfiguring states* (pp. 1-16). Lanham: Rowman & Littlefield.

Hanks, W. F. (1996). *Language und communicative practices*. Boulder: Westview Press.

Hardin, G. (1968). The tragedy of the commons. *Science, 162*(3859), 1243–1248.

Harding, S. (1986). *The science question in feminism*. Ithaca and London: Cornell University Press.

Harmsen, R. (2002). Euroscepticism in the Netherlands: Stirrings of dissent. In R. Harmsen & M. Spiering (Eds.), *Euroscepticism: Party politics, national identity and European integration* (pp. 99–126). Amsterdam: Rodopi.

Harris, P. G. (1999). Common but differentiated responsibility: The kyoto protocol and United States policy. *New York University Environmental Law Journal, 7*(1), 27–48.

Hedahl, M. (2013). Moving from the principle of 'common but differentiated responsibility' to 'equitable access to sustainable development' will aid international climate change negotiations. EUROPP Blog. *London: European politics and policy*. Retrieved March 14, 2014, from http://bit.ly/1bcTR8w.

Henkin, L. (1979). *How nations behave*. New York: Columbia University Press.

Hochstetler, K. (2012). Climate rights and obligations for emerging states: The cases of Brazil and South Africa. *Social Research, 79*(4), 957–982.

Hochstetler, K., & Viola, E. (2012). Brazil and the politics of climate change: Beyond the global commons. *Environmental Politics, 31*(5), 753–771.

Hoffmann, M. J. (2010). Norms and social constructivism in international relations. In R. A. Denemark (Ed.), *International studies online*. Oxford: Blackwell Publishing.

Hoffmann, S. (1986). Hedley bull and his contribution to international relations. *International Affairs, 62*(2), 179–196.

Hofius, M. (2013). *Constituting the EU's Community in the Neighbourhood: The Case of EU Diplomacy. Conference Paper*. Pan-European Conference on International Relations, Warsaw, Poland, 18th–21st of September: European International Studies Association.

Hofius, M. (2014). *Reconstructing Community at the Border: The Case of EU Diplomacy. Unpublished Presentation*. Discourse Analysis: Reconstructive Analysis. Hamburg: University of Hamburg.

Holzscheiter, A. (2011). Power of discourse or discourse of the powerful? The reconstruction of global childhood norms in the drafting of the UN convention on the rights of the child. *Journal of Language and Politics, 10*(1), 1–28.

Hønneland, G. (2011). Kompromiss als Routine Russisch-norwegische Konfliktlösung in der Barentssee. *Osteuropa, 61*(2–3), 257–269.

Hooghe, L., & Marks, G. (1996). *Birth of a Polity: The Struggle Over European Integration. Conference Paper*. Tenth International Conference of Europeanists, Chicago, 14th–16th March 1996.

Howe, B., & Kerby, M. (2009). The Canada-EU turbot war of 1995 and the cybernetic model of decision-making. *The Round Table, 98*(401), 161–179.

Howse, R. (2012). Regulatory measures: SPS, TBT, customs valuation. In A. Narlika, M. Daunton & R. M. Stern (Eds.), *The Oxford handbook on the world trade organization* (pp. 441–457). Oxford: Oxford University Press.

Howse, R., & Teitel, R. (2010). Beyond compliance: Rethinking why international law really matters. *Global Policy, 1*(2), 127–136.

Howse, R., & Teitel, R. (2013). Humanity bounded and unbounded: The regulation of external self-determination under international law. *Law and Ethics of Human Rights, 7*(2), 13–78.

Imig, D. R., & Tarrow, S. G. (2001). *Contentious Europeans: Protest and politics in an emerging polity*. Lanham: Rowman & Littlefield.

Jachtenfuchs, M. (1997). Democracy and governance in the European union. In A. Føllesdal & P. Koslowski (Eds.), *Democracy and the European union* (pp. 37–45). Berlin: Springer.

Jachtenfuchs, M., Diez, T., & Jung, S. (1996). Regieren jenseits der Staatlichkeit? Legitimitätsideen in der Europäischen Union. *Mannheim Working Papers 3*(15), 1–34.

Jachtenfuchs, M., & Kohler-Koch, B. (Eds.). (1996). *Regieren in der Europäischen union*. Opladen: Beck Verlag.

Jackson, R. (2005). *The global convenant. Human conduct in a world of states*. Oxford: Oxford University Press.

Jacobson, D. (1996). *Rights across borders: Immigration and the decline of citizenship*. Baltimore: Johns Hopkins University Press.

Jenkins, P. (2008). Investigating the concepts of legality and legitimacy in sustainable urban development: A case study of land use planning in maputo, mozambique. In S. Sassen (Ed.), *Human settlement development* (Vol. 4, pp. 1–8) Oxford: EOLSS Publishers.

Jenson, J. (1989). Paradigms and political discourse: Protective legislation in France and the United States before 1914. *Canadian Journal of Political Science, 22*(2), 235–258.

Jentoft, S. (2007). Limits of governability: Institutional implications for fisheries and coastal governance. *Marine Policy, 31*(4), 360–370.

Jepperson, R. L., Wendt, A., & Katzenstein, P. J. (1996). Norms, identity, and culture in national security. In P. J. Katzenstein (Ed.), *The culture of national security: norms and identity in world politics* (pp. 33–75). New York: Columbia University Press.

Jessel, A. (2010). *Die Fischereipolitik der EU—ein Netz umstrittener Normen? Magisterarbeit*. Hamburg: University of Hamburg, Chair of Political Science esp Global Governance.

Joyner, C. C., & Alvarez, A. (1996). The turbot war of 1995: lessons for the law of the sea. *The International Journal of Marine and Coastal Law, 11*(4), 425–458.

Kant, I. (1984). *Zum ewigen Frieden*. Ditzingen: Reclam.

Katzenstein, P. (Ed.). (1996). *The culture of national security*. New York: Columbia University Press.

Katzenstein, P., & Sil, R. (2011). De-centering, not discarding, the "Isms": Some friendly amendments. *International Studies Quarterly, 55*(2), 481–485.

Katzenstein, P. J. (1997). *Tamed power: Germany in Europe*. Ithaca, NY: Cornell University Press.

Keck, M. E., & Sikkink, K. (1998). *Activists beyond borders*. Ithaca: Cornell University Press.

Keohane, R. O. (1988). International institutions: Two approaches. *International Studies Quarterly, 32*(4), 379–396.

King, G., Keohane, R. O., & Verba, S. (1994). *Designing social inquiry—scientific inference in qualitative research*. Princeton: Princeton University Press.

Kleingeld, P. (1999). Six varieties of cosmopolitanism in late eighteenth-century Germany. *Journal of the History of Ideas, 60*(3), 505–524.

Koh, H. H. (1997). Why do nations obey international law? *The Yale Law Journal, 106*(8), 2599–2659.

Koh, H. H. (2006). Setting the world right. *The Yale Law Journal, 115*(9), 2350–2379.

Kohler-Koch, B. (1995). The strength of weakness. The transformation of governance in the EU. *Mannheim Working Papers AB 3*(10), 1–22.

Kornprobst, M. (2012). From political judgements to public justifications (and vice versa): how communitites generate reasons upon which to act. *European Journal of International Relations 18*, 1–25. (first published online on July 18).

Krahmann, E. (2007). Transitional states in search of support: PMCs and security sector reform. In S. Chesterman & C. Lehnardt *From mercenaries to market. The rise and regulation of private military companies* (pp. 94–114). Oxford: Oxford University Press.

Krahmann, E. (2010). *States, citizens and the privatization of security*. Cambridge: Cambridge University Press.

Krahmann, E. (2011). Beck and beyond: Selling security in the world risk society. *Review of International Studies, 37*(1), 349–372.

Krasner, S. D. (Ed.). (1983). *International regimes*. Ithaca: Cornell University Press.

Kratochwil, F. (1984). The force of prescriptions. *International Organization, 38*(4), 685–708.

Kratochwil, F. (1989). *Rules, norms, and decisions. On the conditions of practical and legal reasoning in international relations and domestic affairs*. Cambridge: Cambridge University Press.

Kratochwil, F. (2007). Of false promises and good bets: A plea for a pragmatic approach to theory building. *Journal of International Relations and Development, 10*(1), 1–15.

Kratochwil, F. (2012). Leaving sovereignty behind? An inquiry into the politics of post-modernity. In R. Falk, M. Juergensmeyer & V. Popovski (Eds.), *Legality and legitimacy in global affairs* (pp. 127–148). Oxford: Oxford University Press.

Kratochwil, F. (2014). *The status of law in world society. Meditations on the role and rule of law*. Cambridge: Cambridge University Press.

Kratochwil, F., & Ruggie, J. G. (1986). International organization: A state of the art on an art of the state. *International Organization, 40*(4), 753–775.

Krisch, N. (2012). The case for pluralism in postnational law. In G. De Búrca & J. H. H. Weiler (Eds.), *The worlds of European constitutionalism* (pp. 203–261). Cambridge: Cambridge University Press.

Kumm, M., Lang, A. F, Jr., Wiener, A., Tully, J., & Maduro, M. P. (2013). Interdisciplinarity: challenges and opportunities global. *Constitutitonalism - Human Rights, Democracy, and the Rule of Law, 2*(1), 1–5.

Kymlicka, W. (1995). *Multicultural citizenship: A liberal theory of MINORITY rights*. Oxford: Clarendon Press.

Leander, A. (2008). Thinking tools: Analyzing symbolic power and violence. In A. Klotz & D. Prakash (Eds.), *Qualitative methods in international relations: A pluralist guide* (pp. 11–27). Basingstoke: Palgrave.

Lessig, L. (1996). Post: constitutional domains: Democracy, community, managment. *Michigan Law Review, 94*(6), 1422–1470.

Liese, A. (2006). *Staaten am Pranger: Zur Wirkung Internationaler Regime auf Innerstaatliche Menschenrechtspolitik*. Wiesbaden: VS Verlag für Sozialwissenschaften.

Liese, A. (2009). Exceptional necessity: How liberal democracies contest the prohibition of torture and Ill-treatment when countering terrorism. *Journal of International Law and International Relations, 5*(1), 17–48.

Liese, A., & Jetschke, A. (2013). The power of human rights a decade after. from Euphoria to contestation? In T. Risse, K. Sikkink & S. Ropp (Eds.), *The persistent power of human rights* (pp. 26–42). Cambridge: Cambridge University Press.

Linklater, A. (1998). *The transformation of political community*. Columbia: University of South Carolina Press.

Linklater, A. (2007). *Critical theory and world politics. citizenship, sovereignty and humanity*. London: Routledge.

Loader, I., & Walker, N. (2007). *Civilizing security*. Cambridge: Cambridge University Press.

March, J. G., & Olsen, J. P. (1989). *Rediscovering institutions. The organizational basis of politics*. New York: The Free Press.

March, J. G., & Olsen, J. P. (1998). The institutional dynamics of international political orders. *International Organization, 52*(4), 943–969.

Marks, G., Scharpf, F. W., Schmitter, P. C., & Streeck, W. (1996). *Governance in the European union*. London: Sage.

Matthews, D. R. (1996). Mere anarchy? Canada's 'turbot war' as the moral regulation of nature. *The Canadian Journal of Sociology, 21*(4), 505–522.

Melucci, A. (1988). Getting involved: identity and mobilization in social movements. *International Social Movement Research, 1*(1988), 329–348.

Merkel, W., & Petring, A. (2012). Politische Partizipation und Demokratische Inklusion. In T. Mörschel & C. Krell (Eds.), *Demokratie in Deutschland: Zustand-Herausforderungen-Perspektiven* (pp. 93–120). Berlin: Springer VS.

Milliken, J. (1999). The study of discourse in international relations: A critique of research and methods. *European Journal of International Relations, 5*(2), 225–254.

Morris, R. T. (1956). A typology of norms. *American Sociological Review, 21*(5), 610–613.

Müller, H. (1994). Internationale Beziehungen als Kommunikatives Handeln. Zur Kritik der Utilitaristischen Handlungstheorien. *Zeitschrift für Internationale Beziehungen, 1*(1), 15–44.

Müller, H. (2001). International relations as communicative action. In K. M. Fierke & K. E. Jørgensen (Eds.), *Constructing international relations. The next generation* (pp. 160–178). Armonk, NY: M.E. Sharpe.

Müller, H. (2004). Arguing, bargaining and all that: Communicative action, rationalist theory and the logic of appropriateness in international relations. *European Journal of International Relations, 10*(3), 395–435.

Müller, H., & Wunderlich, C. (Eds.). (2013). *Norm dynamics in multilateral arms control. interests, conflicts, and justice*. Athens: University of Georgia Press.

Neyer, J. (2012). *The justification of Europe: A political theory of supranational integration*. Oxford: Oxford University Press.

Nicholson, L. J. (Ed.). (1997). *The second wave: A reader in feminist theory*. London: Routledge.

Onuf, N. (1989). *World of our making: Rules and rule in social theory and international relations*. Columbia: University of South Carolina Press.

Onuf, N. (1994). The constitution of international society. *European Journal of International Law, 5*(1), 1–19.

Onuf, N. (2013). Making sense, making worlds. Constructivism in social theory and international relations. Abingdon: Routledge.

Ørebech, P. (2013). *The Decision-Making is All that Matters: How Fisheries is Caught up in a Top-down Regulatory Labyrinth. Conference Paper (on file with the author)*. International Studies Association Conference, San Francisco, 4 April 2013, Retrieved March 14, 2014, from http://files.isanet.org/ConferenceArchive/1bb244905bd547c5b6572f5d67079271.pdf.

Ostrom, E. (1990). *Governing the commons: The evolution of institutions for collective actions.* Cambridge: Cambridge University Press.

Owen, D. (2007). Self-government and 'democracy as reflexive co-operation'. Reflections on honneth's social and political ideal. In B. van den Brink & D. Owen (Eds.), *Recognition and power. Axel Honneth and the tradition of critical social theory* (pp. 290–320). Cambridge: Cambridge University Press.

Owen, D. (2011). Foucault, Tully and agonistic struggles over recognition. In M. Bankovsky & A. Le Goff (Eds.), *Recognition theory and contemporary French moral and political philosophy* (pp. 133–165). Manchester: Manchester University Press.

Park, S., & Vetterlein, A. (2010). *Owning development: Creating global policy norms in the IMF and the world bank.* Cambridge: Cambridge University Press.

Pettit, P. (1997). *Republicanism—a theory of freedom and government.* Oxford: Oxford University Press.

Pogge, T. (2009). *Gerechtigkeit in der Einen welt. Philosophy meets politics.* Essen: Klartext Verlagsgesellschaft.

Powell, W. W., & DiMaggio, P. (Eds.). (1991). *The new institutionalism in organizational analysis.* Chicago: University of Chicago Press.

Price, R., & Reus-Smit, C. (1998). Dangerous liaisons? Critical international theory and constructivism. *European Journal of International Relations, 4*(3), 259–294.

Rawls, J. (1971). *A theory of justice.* Cambridge, MA: The Belknap Press of Harvard University Press.

Rawls, J. (2002). *The law of peoples.* Cambridge, MA: Harvard University Press.

Reus-Smit, C. (1997). The constitutional structure of international society and the nature of fundamental institutions. *International Organization, 51*(4), 555–589.

Reus-Smit, C. (2001). Human rights and the social construction of sovereignty. *Review of International Studies, 27*(4), 519–538.

Reus-Smit, C. (2013). *Individual rights and the making of international system.* Cambridge: Cambridge University Press.

Risse, T. (2000). 'Let's Argue!': Communicative action in world politics. *International Organization, 54*(1), 1–39.

Risse, T., & Kleine, M. (2010). Deliberation in negotiations. *Journal of European Public Policy, 17*(5), 708–726.

Risse, T., Ropp, S., & Sikkink, K. (1999). *The power of human rights: International norms and domestic change.* Cambridge: Cambridge University Press.

Rittberger, V., & Mayer, P. (1993). *Regime theory and international relations.* Oxford and New York: Clarendon Press.

Rosenau, J. N., & Czempiel, E.-O. (1992). *Governance without government: Order and change in world politics.* Cambridge: Cambridge University Press.

Rosert, E. (2012). Fest Etabliert und weiterhin Lebendig: Normenforschung in den Internationalen Beziehungen. *Zeitschrift für Politikwissenschaft, 22*(4), 599–623.

Ruggie, J. G. (1992). Multilateralism: The anatomy of an institution. *International Organization, 46*(3), 561–598.

Ruggie, J. G. (1998). *Constructing the world polity: Essays on international institutionalization.* London: Routledge.

Ruggie, J. G. (2005). Global markets and global governance: The prospects for convergence. In S. Bernstein & L. W. Pauly (Eds.), *Global governance: Towards a new grand compromise?* (pp. 23–50). Albany: State University Press of New York.

Sandholtz, W. (2008). Dynamics of international norm change: Rules against wartime plunder. *European Journal of International Relations, 14*(1), 101–131.

Sands, P. (2006). *Lawless world—the whistle-blowing account of how bush and blair are taking the law into their own hands.* London: Penguin Books.

Schaefer, A. (1995/96, 1995). Canada-Spain fishing dispute (the turbot war). *Georgetown International Environmental Law Review 8*(3), 437–449.

Scharpf, F. W. (1997). *Games real actors play: Actor-centered institutionalism in policy research*. Boulder: Westview Press.

Schimmelfennig, F. (2000). International socialization in the new Europe: Rational action in an institutional environment. *European Journal of International Relations, 6*(1), 109–139.

Schwellnus, G. (2006). Reasons for constitutionalization: Non-discrimination, minority rights and social rights in the convention on the EU charter of fundamental rights. *Journal of European Public Policy, 13*(8), 1265–1283.

Scott, J. (2002). Flexibility, 'proceduralization', and environmental governance. In G. d. Búrca & J. Scott (Eds.), *Constitutional change in the EU. From uniformity to flexibility?* (pp. 259–297). Oxford: Hart Publishing.

Scott, J., & Trubek, D. M. (2002). Mind the gap: Law and new approaches to governance in the European union. *European Law Journal, 8*(1), 1–18.

Scott, J. W. (1988). *Gender and the politics of history*. New York: Columbia University Press.

Searle, J. (1995). *The construction of social reality*. New York: Free Press.

Sen, A. (2009). *The idea of justice*. London: Penguin Books.

Sending, O. J., & Neumann, I. B. (2011). Banking on power: How some practices in an international organization anchor others. In E. Adler & V. Pouliot (Eds.), *International practices* (pp. 231–254). Cambridge: Cambridge University Press.

Senge, K. (2013). Corporate Social Responsibility als Legitimationsprinzip von Unternehmen in der World Polity. Ph.D. Thesis. Faculty of Economical and Social Science. Hamburg: University of Hamburg.

Shapcott, R. (2001). *Justice, community and dialogue in international relations*. Cambridge: Cambridge University Press.

Slaughter, A.-M. (2004). *A new world order*. Princeton: Princeton University Press.

Slaughter, A.-M. (2005). Security, solidarity, and sovereignty: The grand themes of UN reform. *American Journal of International Law, 99*(3), 619–631.

Slaughter, A. M., & Burke-White, W. (2002). An international constitutional moment. *Harvard International Law Journal, 43*(1), 1–21.

Soysal, Y. N. (1994). *The limits of citizenship migrants and postnational membership in France*. Chicago: University of Chicago Press.

Stone, C. D. (2004). Common but differentiated responsibilities in international law. *The American Journal of International Law, 98*(2), 276–301.

Tamanaha, B. Z. (2004). *On the rule of law. History, politics, theory*. Cambridge: Cambridge University Press.

Tarrow, S., Tilly, C., & McAdam, D. (2001). *Dynamics of contention*. Cambridge: Cambridge University Press.

Taylor, C. (1991). *The ethics of authenticity*. Cambridge, MA: Harvard University Press.

Taylor, C. (1993). To follow a rule. In C. Calhoun, E. LiPuma & M. Postone (Eds.), *Bourdieu: Critical perspectives* (pp. 45–60). Cambridge: Polity Press.

Teitel, R. (2013). *Humanity's law*. Oxford: Oxford University Press.

Tilly, C. (Ed.). (1975). *The formation of national states in Western Europe*. Princeton: Princeton University Press.

Toope, S. J. (2000). Emerging patterns of governance and international law. In: M. Byers (Ed.), *The role of law in international politics* (pp. 91–108). Oxford: Oxford University Press.

Toope, S. J. (2003). *International law and international relations*. Toronto: University of Toronto, Faculty of Law.

Tully, J. (1993). *An approach to political philosophy: Locke in context*. Cambridge: Cambridge University Press.

Tully, J. (1995). *Strange multiplicity: Constitutionalism in an age of diversity*. Cambridge: Cambridge University Press.

Tully, J. (2000). Struggles over recognition and distribution. *Constellations, 7*(4), 469–482.

Tully, J. (2002). The unfreedom of the moderns in comparison to their ideals of constitutional democracy. *The Modern Law Review, 65*(2), 204–228.

Tully, J. (2008a). *Public philosophy in a new key* (Vol. 1). Cambridge: Cambridge University Press.

Tully, J. (2008b). *Public philosophy in a new key* (Vol. 2). Cambridge: Cambridge University Press.

Tully, J., & Gagnon, A.-G. (Eds.). (2001). *Multinational democracies.* Cambridge: Cambridge University Press.

Vogt, D. (2010). Brian tobin and the turbot war of 1995, Humanities 360°, Andover, MA: Helium Publishing. Retrieved March 19, 2014, from http://www.humanities360.com/index.php/brian-tobin-and-the-turbot-war-of-1995-19910/.

Waever, O. (1996). European security identities. *Journal of Common Market Studies, 34*(1), 103–132.

Waldron, J. (2006). Cosmopolitan norms. In R. Post (Ed.), *Another cosmopolitanism. The berkeley tanner lectures* (pp. 83–101). Oxford: Oxford University Press.

Walker, N. (2003). Constitutionalising enlargement, enlarging constitutionalism. *European Law Journal, 9*(3), 365–385.

Waltz, K. N. (1979). *Theory of international politics.* New York: McGraw-Hill.

Weber, C. (1994). Good girls, little girls, and bad girls—male paranoia in Robert Keohane's critique of feminist international relations. *Millennium Journal of International Studies, 23*(2), 337–349.

Weldes, J., & Saco, D. (1996). Making state action possible: The United States and the discursive construction of 'The Cuban Problem', 1960–1994. *Millennium: Journal of International Studies, 25*(2), 361–395.

Wendt, A. (1994). Collective identity formation and the international state. *American Political Science Review, 88*(2), 84–96.

Wendt, A. (1999). *Social theory of international politics.* Cambridge: Cambridge University Press.

Wendt, A. (2003). Why a world state is inevitable. *European Journal of International Relations, 9*(4), 491–542.

Wenger, E. (1998). *Communities of practice: Learning, meaning, and identity.* Cambridge: Cambridge University Press.

Whitworth, S. (1989). Gender and the inter-paradigm debate. *Millennium, 18*(2), 265–272.

Wiener, A. (2003). Towards a Transnational Nomos—The Role of Institutions in the Process of Constitutionalization, *Jean Monnet Working Paper—Symposium: European Integration—The New German Scholarship* 09/2003, pp. 1–34.

Wiener, A. (2004). Contested compliance: Interventions on the normative structure of world politics. *European Journal of International Relations, 10*(2), 189–234.

Wiener, A. (2007). The dual quality of norms and governance beyond the state: sociological and normative approaches to interaction. *Critical Review of International Social and Political Philosophy, 10*(1), 47–69.

Wiener, A. (2008). *The invisible constitution of politics: Contested norms and international encounters.* Cambridge: Cambridge University Press.

Wiener, A. (2009). Enacting meaning-in-use. Qualitative research on norms and international relations. *Review of International Studies, 35*(1), 175–193.

Wiener, A., Vetterlein, A., & Hansen-Magnusson, H. (2012). *An interactive approach to global governance: Stakeholdership and knowledge.* Hamburg: University of Hamburg. (unpublished research proposal, on file with author).

Wiener, A., & Oeter, S. (2011). *Constitutionalism unbound: introducing theoretical triangulation for international relations.* Hamburg: University of Hamburg; Science Foundation of the Hamburg Senate. (Unpublished Research Proposal).

Wiener, A., & Puetter, U. (2009). The quality of norms is what actors make of it: Constructivist research on norms. *Journal of International Law and International Relations, 5*(1), 1–16.

Wiener, A., & Schwellnus, G. (2004). Contested norms in the process of EU enlargement: Non-discrimination and minority rights. In G. Berman & K. Pistor (Eds.), *Law and governance in an enlarged European union* (pp. 451–484). Oxford: Hart Publishing.

Wiener, A., & Vetterlein, A. (2011). *Theorizing contested norms in fisheries governance: Communication gaps and organising principles* (pp. 1–18). Hamburg: University of Hamburg. (Unpublished Research Proposal).

Young, O. R. (1991). Political leadership and regime formation: On the development of institutions in international society. *International Organization, 45*(3), 281–308.

Zalewski, M. (1996). 'All these theories yet the bodies keep piling up': Theories, theorists, theorising. In S. Smith, K. Booth & M. Zalewski (Eds.), *International theory: Positivism and beyond* (pp. 340–353). Cambridge: Cambridge University Press.

Zimmermann, L., von Staden, A., Marciniak, A., Wallbott, L., & Arndt, F. (2013). Muss Ordnung sein? Zum Umgang mit Konflikten zwischen normativen Ordnungen. *Zeitschrift für Internationale Beziehungen, 20*(1), 35–60.

Zumbansen, P. (2012). Comparative, global and transnational constitutionalism: The emergence of a transnational legal-pluralist order. *Global Constitutionalism, 1*(1), 16–52.

Zürn, M. (2000). Democratic governance beyond the nation-state: The EU and other international institutions. *European Journal of International Relations, 6*(2), 183–221.

Zürn, M., Binder, M., & Ecker-Ehrhardt, M. (2012). International authority and its politicization. *International Theory, 4*(1), 69–106.

Zürn, M., Nollkaemper, A., & Peerenboom, R. (Eds.). (2012). *Rule of law dynamics—in an era of international and transnational governance.* Cambridge: Cambridge University Press.

Printed in Great Britain
by Amazon